Spelling

Games and Activities

GRADE 3

Content Development: Tiffany Hailey
Kathleen Jorgensen
Lisa Vitarisi Mathews
Copy Editing: Laurie Westrich
Art Direction: Yuki Meyer
Illustration: Bryan Langdo
Mary Rojas
Cover Design: Yuki Meyer
Design/Production: Paula Acojido
Yuki Meyer
Jessica Onken

EMC 8273

**Congratulations on your
purchase of some of the
finest teaching materials
in the world.**

For information about other Evan-Moor products, call 1-800-777-4362,
fax 1-800-777-4332, or visit our website, www.evan-moor.com.
Entire contents © 2023 Evan-Moor Corporation
10 Harris Court, Suite C-3, Monterey, CA 93940-5773. Printed in USA.

CPSIA: Sheridan Saline, Inc., Saline, MI, USA [10/2023]

Contents

Themed Units

Extra Practice Worksheets 91

What's in *Spelling Games and Activities*

Support for Writing

Spelling skills are essential for children to practice in order to communicate well in writing. Many people rely on technology to fix their spelling, but technology can only guess what the writer means. Spelling must be accurate to be understood. Even though there are many spelling rules and even more exceptions, spelling practice can help students understand those rules and apply them to their writing.

Spelling Games and Activities gives you two ways to help your students practice spelling:

- the engaging themed unit section, which brings together related words in grade-appropriate contexts in fun and interesting ways

- the extra practice worksheets section, which uses words from Evan-Moor's *Building Spelling Skills* series and can be used to enrich those lessons or on its own

8 Themed Units

Spelling Games and Activities offers 8 units of grade-level topics that engage students and provide context for practicing spelling useful words. Each unit introduces 15 theme-related words along with the spelling patterns and rules that are used in those words. The unit continues with fun puzzles, cutouts, and other activities to practice writing and spelling the words, followed by a game or other special activity done as a class or in small groups.

Unit Features

You can assign all the pages in a cohesive unit or choose individual worksheets as needed to support your spelling program or to reinforce words learned in other content areas. Each 10-page unit provides a set of spelling words and related spelling tips, a variety of activity pages, and a game or project with teacher directions.

Unit Overview

An introduction telling students what the unit's words have in common, along with the words themselves

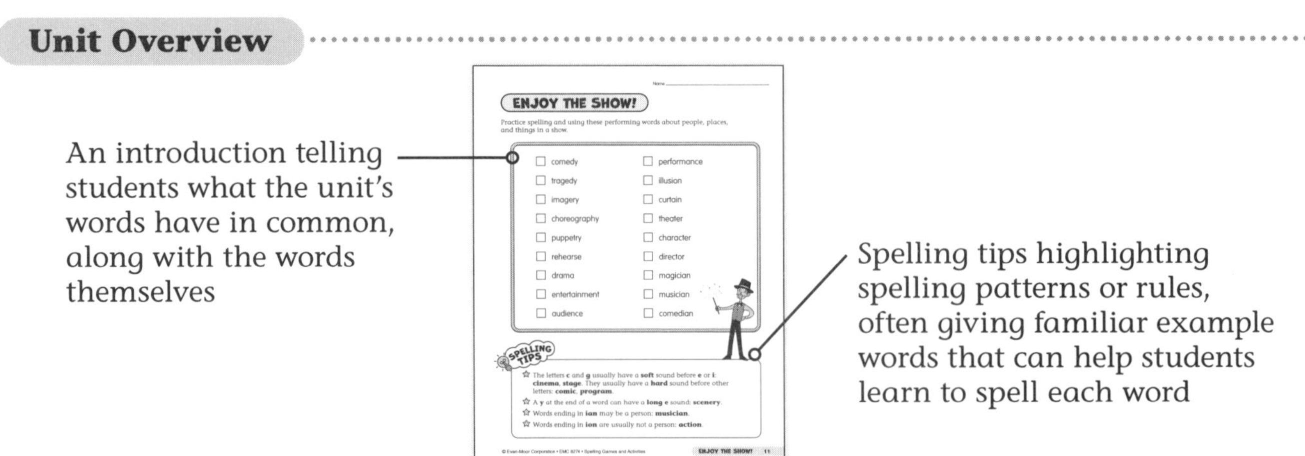

Spelling tips highlighting spelling patterns or rules, often giving familiar example words that can help students learn to spell each word

    Spelling Games and Activities • EMC 8273 • © Evan-Moor Corporation

Theme-Based Activity Pages

There are a wide variety of theme-based activities in every theme unit. These are some examples.

Use phonics clues

Students use sound clues to write a spelling word that completes a sentence.

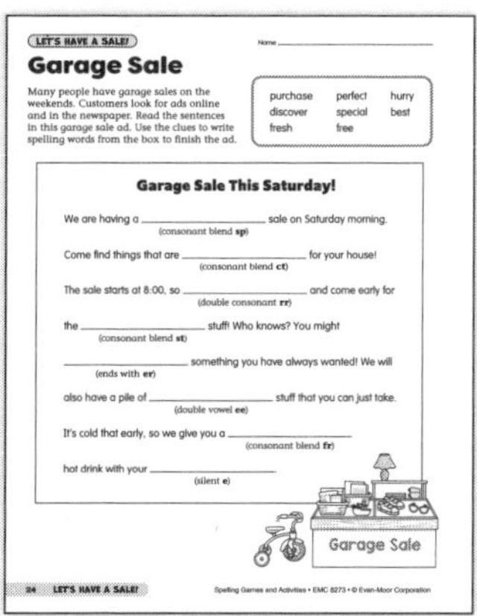

Solve riddles

Students finish rhyming riddles that give clues to the missing spelling word.

Complete words

Students supply missing letters in pairs of words and then figure out how the words are similar.

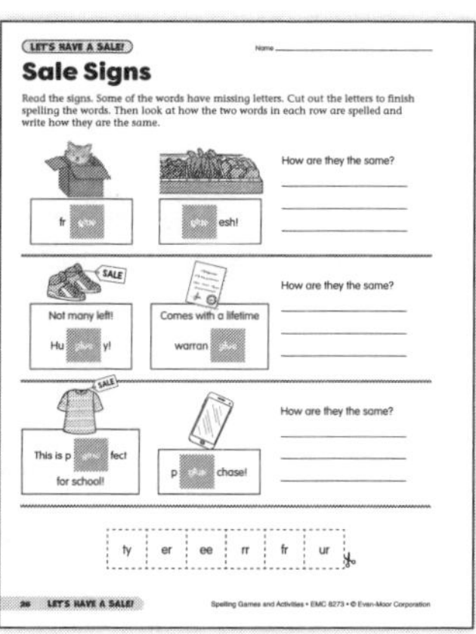

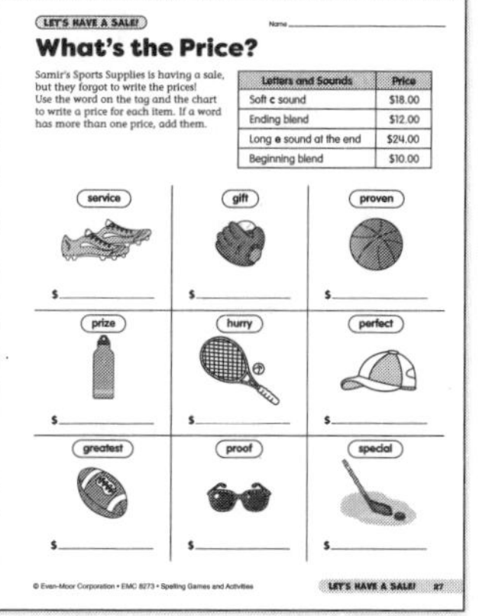

Analyze words

Students listen for certain sounds or structures in words and give them a value.

Game, Activity, or Hands-on Center

A fun theme-related game, often a variation of a familiar children's game, lets students practice their words in a small or large group setting.

A page of instructions and materials for the teacher is included, as well as any cards or game boards.

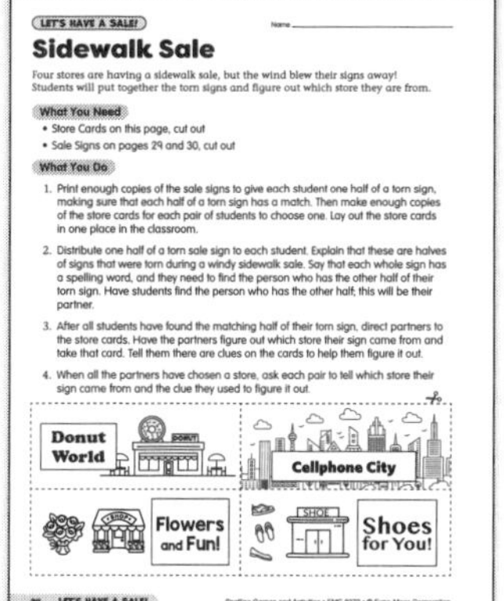

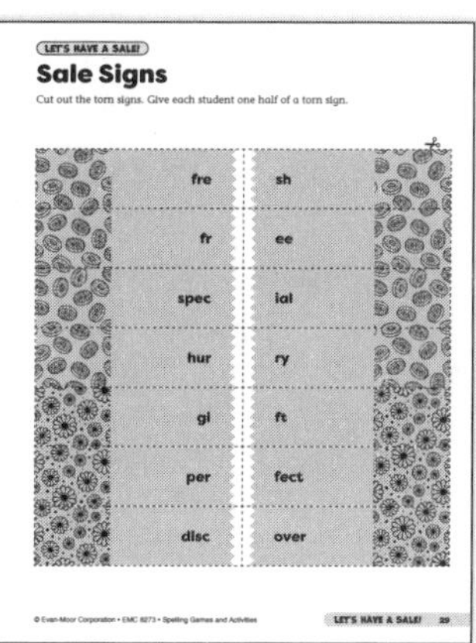

What's in *Spelling Games and Activities*, continued

Extra Practice Worksheets

Students apply the same spelling tips from the themed units to sets of words from *Building Spelling Skills*. These pages can be used independently or with any spelling series.

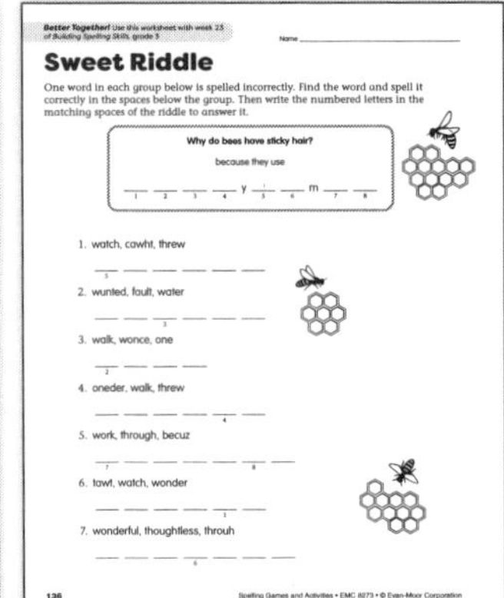

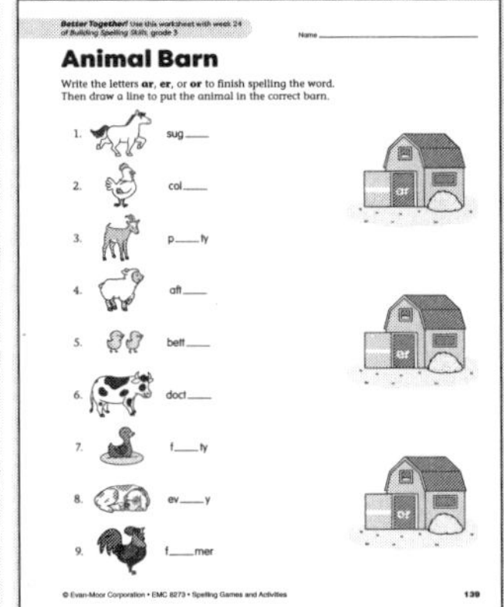

Additional Resources

Spelling Strategies

A variety of useful strategies that help students learn a word's spelling by analyzing sounds and word structures or by using dictionary skills and memory aids

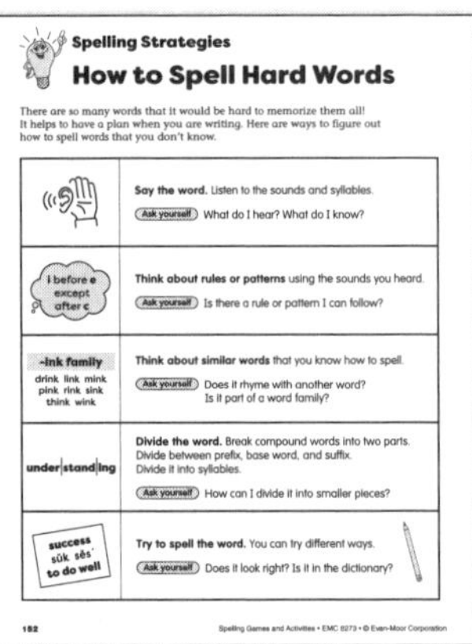

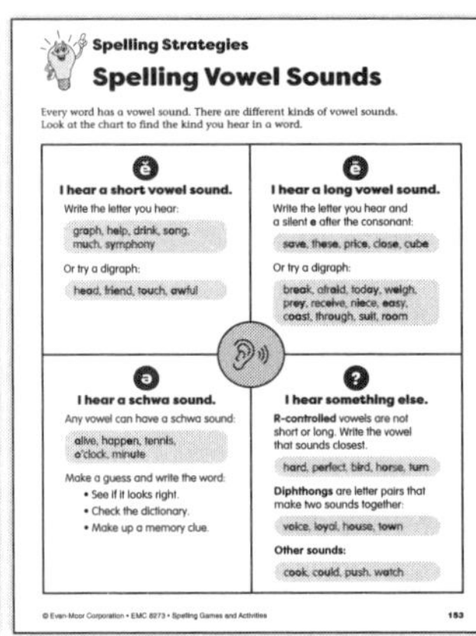

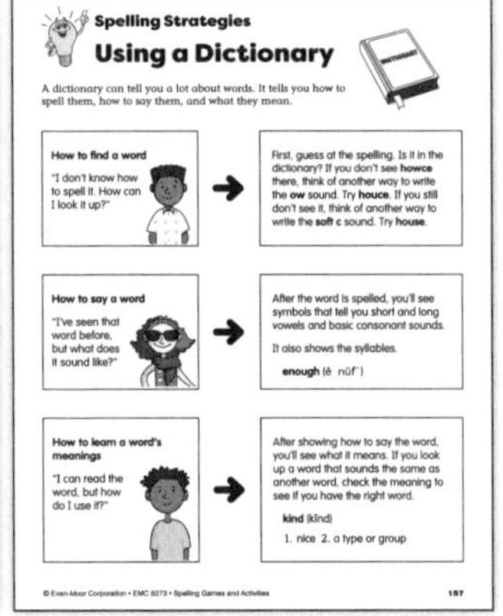

Spelling Word List

Alphabetized glossary of all spelling words in the book

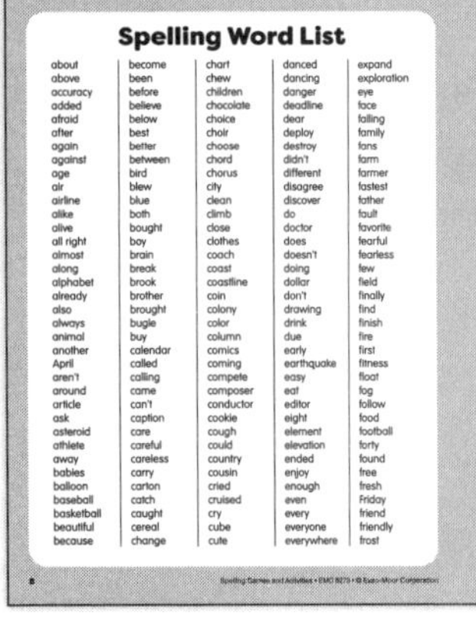

Answer Key

Provided for any page that has student answers. The correct answer or a sample response is shown, unless the question is completely open-ended.

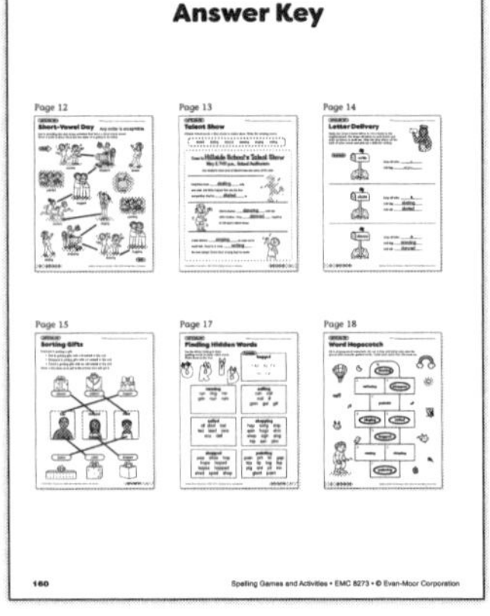

How to Use *Spelling Games and Activities*

Flexible Use

Decide which pages you will use. You can use an entire unit from the themed section, pages focusing on a particular skill, or extra practice pages that apply skills to different words. Then print copies for your students. It is recommended that you include the introduction page that provides helpful spelling tips for the skills you're working on.

Connections to Other Subjects

The units in this book were chosen to represent common experiences of children in third grade, along with general grade-level words. These topics may relate to other subjects you are teaching and could augment other lessons. For example, Let's Have a Sale! and Where To? could be used with social studies lessons focusing on basic economics and geography. World of Science and Space Adventure could extend a science lesson about air, animals, the night sky, or technology. Ready, Set, Go! could be used when students must spend recess inside on a rainy day. Use any set of spelling words with a handwriting lesson for extra practice in both.

Extend the Challenge or the Words

If you find an activity or game particularly useful, feel free to use it as a template for other sets of spelling words or other features of the same words. For example, the activity on page 43 asks students to give points to words based on the type of **e** sound in the word. You could use the same point chart with different words. You could also award points for different sounds in the same words, such as short **a**, short **e**, short **i**, and short **o**.

Use the Extra Practice Worksheets

If you want additional practice on specific skills or want students to practice applying skills to a new set of words, use pages from the extra practice section. This section features all the spelling words from Evan-Moor's *Building Spelling Skills* weekly lessons. If you are using *Building Spelling Skills*, you can use these extra practice worksheets to enhance your weekly lessons, giving students more practice with the same words.

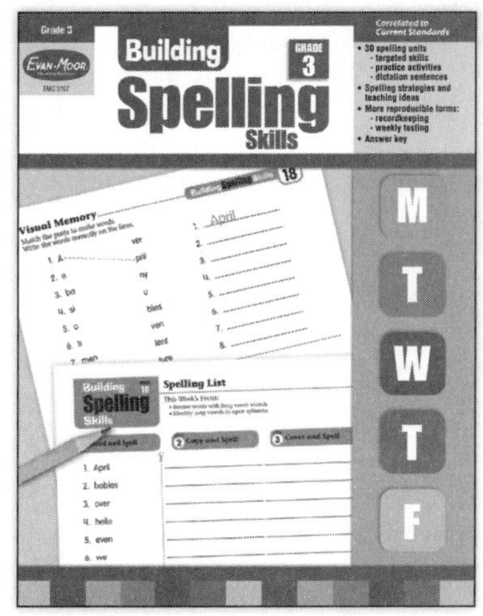

Spelling Word List

about	become	chart	danced	expand
above	been	chew	dancing	exploration
accuracy	before	children	danger	eye
added	believe	chocolate	deadline	face
afraid	below	choice	dear	falling
after	best	choir	deploy	family
again	better	choose	destroy	fans
against	between	chord	didn't	farm
age	bird	chorus	different	farmer
air	blew	city	disagree	fastest
airline	blue	clean	discover	father
alike	both	climb	do	fault
alive	bought	close	doctor	favorite
all right	boy	clothes	does	fearful
almost	brain	coach	doesn't	fearless
along	break	coast	doing	few
alphabet	brook	coastline	dollar	field
already	brother	coin	don't	finally
also	brought	colony	drawing	find
always	bugle	color	drink	finish
animal	buy	column	due	fire
another	calendar	comics	early	first
April	called	coming	earthquake	fitness
aren't	calling	compete	easy	float
around	came	composer	eat	fog
article	can't	conductor	editor	follow
ask	caption	cookie	eight	food
asteroid	care	cough	element	football
athlete	careful	could	elevation	forty
away	careless	country	ended	found
babies	carry	cousin	enjoy	free
balloon	carton	cried	enough	fresh
baseball	catch	cruise	even	Friday
basketball	caught	cry	every	friend
beautiful	cereal	cube	everyone	friendly
because	change	cute	everywhere	frost

fuel
full
funniest
future
galaxy
getting
ghost
giant
gift
girl
give
given
gnat
gnaw
gone
good
goose
graph
great
greatest
ground
group
grow
grown
guard
guess
habitat
half
handball
happened
happening
happier
happiest
happily
happiness
hard
harmony
have
having

head
headline
heard
hello
help
here
high
hold
homework
horse
hospital
hour
house
huge
hugged
hugging
human
hurry
I
I'll
I'm
insect
interview
into
invention
it's
joined
joked
journey
joyful
jury
kind
knew
knight
knot
know
ladies
lady
laid

large
learn
leave
left
leisure
let's
letter
liar
life
light
limb
live
location
longer
looked
lower
loyal
lullaby
machine
magnet
mall
mammal
many
marathon
maybe
mean
measure
melody
menu
middle
might
minute
missed
Mississippi
money
more
morning
most
mother

move
much
music
musical
my
myself
nation
near
neighbor
nephew
new
next
nice
niece
night
north
number
nurse
o'clock
odor
of
often
oily
once
one
only
open
opinion
opponent
orbit
orphan
other
our
outside
over
overseas
own
oyster
painted

painting
partner
party
passenger
pattern
peace
people
perfect
performer
phone
photograph
pickleball
piece
pitch
planet
playing
please
pocket
pointing
poison
pollen
practice
presents
pretty
prey
price
prize
problem
proof
proofreader
proven
publisher
purchase
push
put
quickly
quietly
raise
reached

read
received
recital
rehearsal
relaxation
remember
reporter
reptile
rewrap
right
road trip
roam
robot
rocket
room
rough
running
said
save
school
sea
search
seen
service
sew
she
shield
shoes
shopped
shopping
short
should
show
shy
sightseeing
silent
singing
skateboard
skated

skating
slowly
small
smarter
smiled
smiling
smog
snap
soccer
softball
some
something
song
songwriter
soup
source
spaceship
spacesuit
special
spelling
stand
stare
start
started
station
stayed
still
stirred
stood
story
straight
straw
strongest
studied
study
such
sugar
sure
surprise

surprises
swam
swim
swimming
symphony
takes
taught
teacher
teammate
telescope
tennis
than
that's
their
there
thermometer
they
they're
think
those
thoughtless
three
threw
throne
through
tiny
tired
to
today
together
told
too
touch
tough
town
toys
transportation
tried
true

truth
try
turned
two
typesetter
under
unhappy
uniform
unit
universe
unknown
until
unwrap
upon
use
used
useful
useless
usually
vacation
very
voice
volleyball
voyage
wait
walk
wanted
warning
warranty
watch
water
waved
way
we
wear
weather
weight
were
we're

where
which
while
white
who
whole
why
willing
winner
with
without
wonder
wonderful
won't
word
work
world
worthless
would
wouldn't
wrapper
write
writing
written
wrong
wrote
year
you
young
your
you're
zipper

LET'S DO IT!

Practice spelling and using these action words that name different things to do.

- ☐ painting
- ☐ painted
- ☐ calling
- ☐ called
- ☐ skating
- ☐ skated
- ☐ dancing
- ☐ danced

- ☐ shopping
- ☐ shopped
- ☐ hugging
- ☐ hugged
- ☐ singing
- ☐ running
- ☐ writing

SPELLING TIPS

⭐ The **-ed** and **-ing** endings show when an action is happening. The -ed ending can have a **d** sound, a **t** sound, or an **ǝd** sound. Examples: **played**, **jumped**, **acted**

⭐ If a word ends with two consonants or a long vowel sound, just add the **-ed** or **-ing** ending. Examples: **talk**, **talked**, **talking**; **show**, **showed**, **showing**

⭐ If a word ends with a **silent e**, drop the **e** before adding the ending. Examples: **bake**, **baked**, **baking**

⭐ If a word ends with a short vowel and one consonant, double the consonant and add the ending. Examples: **jog**, **jogged**, **jogging**

Name ______________________

Short-Vowel Day

Jun is spending the day doing activities that have a short vowel sound.
Draw a path to show what Jun has done or is going to do today.

Spelling Games and Activities • EMC 8273 • © Evan-Moor Corporation

Name ____________________

Talent Show

Hillside School made a flier about its talent show. Write the missing words.

skated   skating   danced   dancing   singing   writing

Come to **Hillside School's Talent Show**
May 2, 7:00 p.m., School Auditorium

Our students have a lot of talent! Here are some of the acts:

Kenji has been ________________ only one year. His tricks helped him win the first competition that he ________________ in.

Marta started ________________ with her older brother. They ________________ together in last year's talent show.

Caleb started ________________ as soon as he could talk. Now he is even ________________ his own songs! Come hear a song that he wrote.

Name ___________________

Letter Delivery

Linda the Letter Carrier drives to every home in her neighborhood. She drops off letters to each home and picks up letters to mail out. Help her drop letters off the ends of some words and pick up a different ending.

Example

Drop off letter: _______ e _______

Add **ing**: _______ writing _______

Drop off letter: _______________

Add **ing**: _______________

Add **ed**: _______________

Drop off letter: _______________

Add **ing**: _______________

Add **ed**: _______________

   Spelling Games and Activities • EMC 8273 • © Evan-Moor Corporation

Sorting Gifts

Everyone is getting a gift!

- Dad is getting gifts with a **d sound** at the end.
- Margaret is getting gifts with a **t sound** at the end.
- David is getting gifts with an **ǝd sound** at the end.

Draw a line from each gift to the person who will get it.

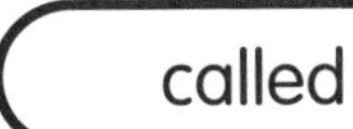

Name ___________________

Write to Someone

Write a letter to a friend or family member. Tell what you have been doing. Use at least 5 spelling words.

skated	skating	danced	dancing	called	calling
painted	painting	shopped	shopping	hugged	hugging
running	singing	writing			

Finding Hidden Words

Use the letters hiding in these spelling words to make other words. Write them in the box.

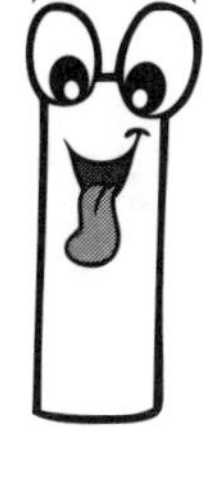

Example

hugged

huge   egg   dug

due   hue

running

calling

called

shopping

shopped

painting

Name _______________

Word Hopscotch

Ali is playing word hopscotch. He has to hop and jump only onto the spaces with correctly spelled words. Circle each space that Ali lands on.

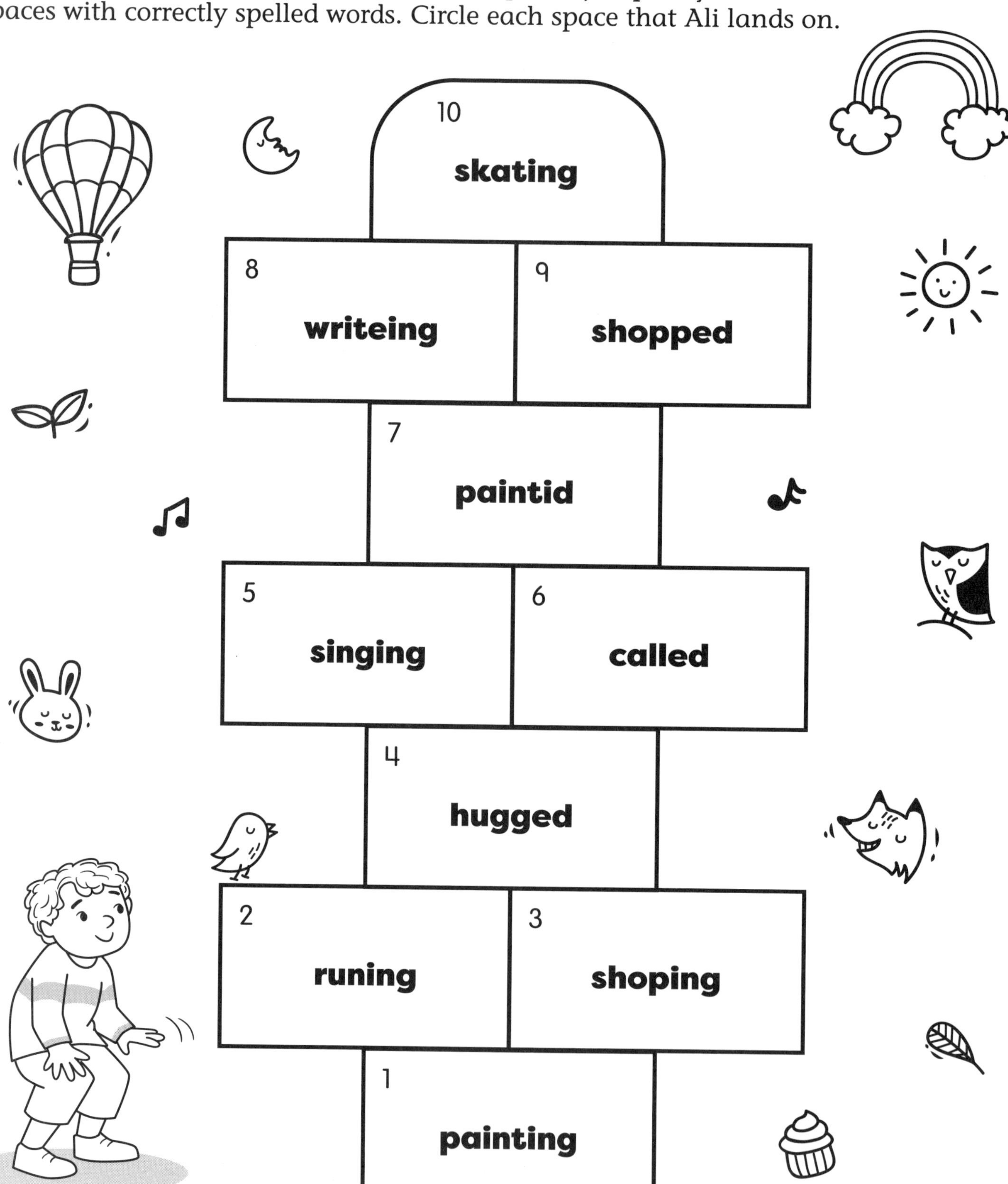

Spelling Games and Activities • EMC 8273 • © Evan-Moor Corporation

Name ___________________________

Act It Out

Students guess what action their teammates are acting out.

What You Need

- Action Cards on page 20
- whiteboard
- whiteboard marker
- die

How to Play

The object of the game is to act out, guess, and spell as many spelling words as you can for your team.

1. Divide the class into 2 teams and have each team sit or stand together. Lay out the action cards facedown on a table, all separate.

2. Choose one player from each team to be the first actor. Have one of the actors choose an action card and show it to the other actor and to the teacher. No one should say the word.

3. When the teacher says, "Lights, camera, action!" both actors act out the action for their teammates. They can make any movements but may not talk or make other sounds.

4. Teammates can call out the word that they think is being acted out. The first person who guesses correctly rolls the die to see how many points the team earns. The teacher records the points on the whiteboard. Then the teacher chooses someone from the other team to spell the word. If spelled correctly, that student rolls the die to see how many points that team earns. The teacher records the points on the whiteboard.

5. Continue until all remaining action cards have been used, choosing a new actor from each team for every card.

Action Cards

writing 	**painting** 	**calling** 
running 	**dancing** 	**singing** 
shopping 	**hugging** 	**skating** 

LET'S HAVE A SALE!

Practice spelling and using these words about buying and selling.

- ☐ fresh
- ☐ free
- ☐ gift
- ☐ prize
- ☐ proven
- ☐ proof
- ☐ special
- ☐ best

- ☐ hurry
- ☐ warranty
- ☐ service
- ☐ purchase
- ☐ perfect
- ☐ discover
- ☐ greatest

SPELLING TIPS

★ A vowel before an **r** changes its sound from short or long to **r-controlled.** Example: **worth**

★ The letter pairs **fr**, **gr**, **pr**, **st**, **ft**, and **ct** are **consonant blends**. Consonant blends have two or more sounds that are said together. Examples: **great**, **product**

★ When you divide a word with **double consonants** into syllables, split between the double consonants. Examples: **shopping = shop | ping, borrow = bor | row**

Name ______________________

Store Signs

Read the store signs. Then look at the chart on page 23.
Write the big word from each sign in the correct column on the chart.

Hint: You may write some words in more than one column.

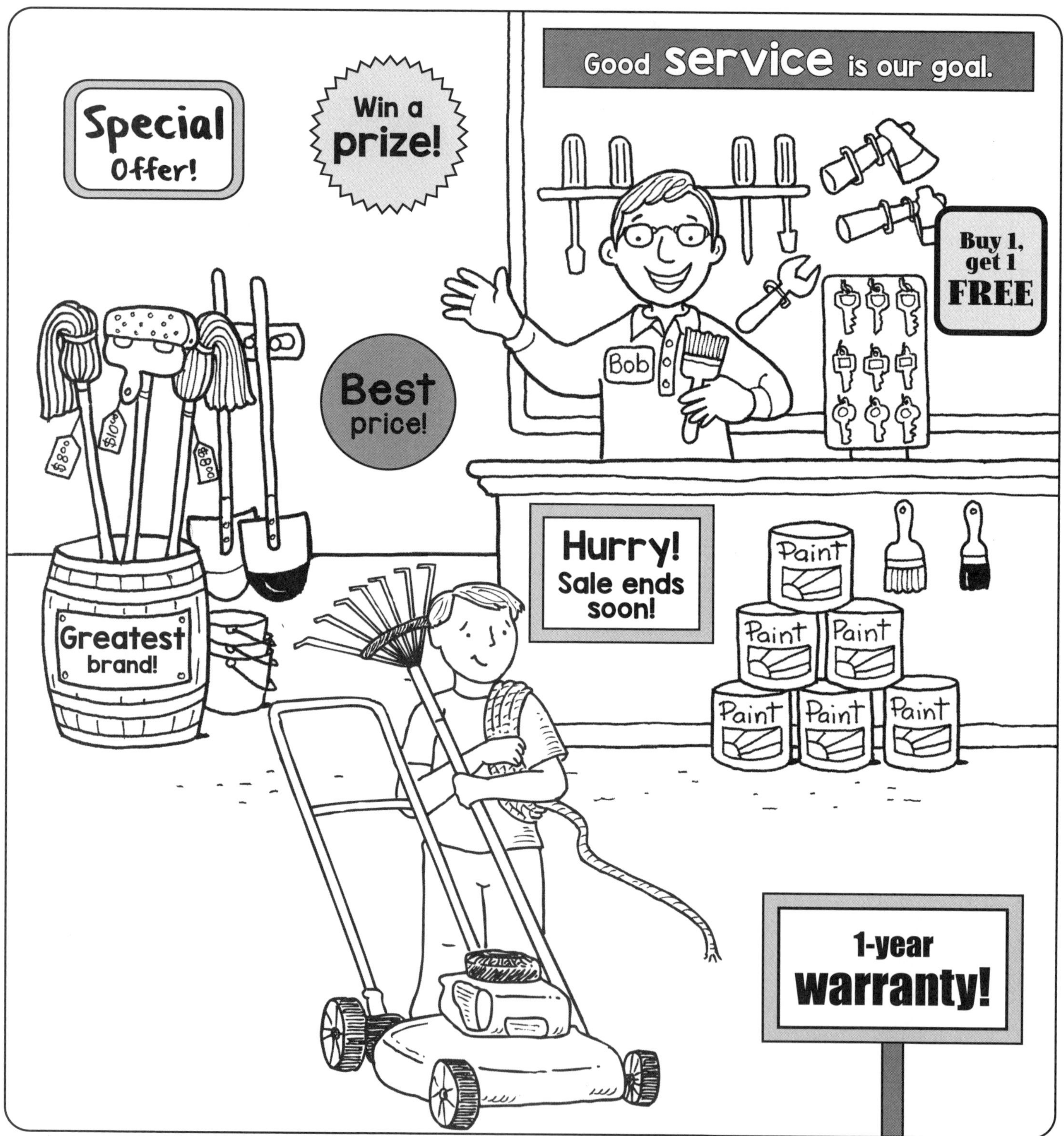

    Spelling Games and Activities • EMC 8273 • © Evan-Moor Corporation

Name ___________________________

Store Signs, *continued*

Store Signs Words Chart

double consonants	consonant blend	r-controlled vowel

Garage Sale

Name _______________________

Many people have garage sales on the weekends. Customers look for ads online and in the newspaper. Read the sentences in this garage sale ad. Use the clues to write spelling words from the box to finish the ad.

purchase	perfect	hurry
discover	special	best
fresh	free	

Garage Sale This Saturday!

We are having a ________________________ sale on Saturday morning.
(consonant blend **sp**)

Come find things that are ________________________ for your house!
(consonant blend **ct**)

The sale starts at 8:00, so ________________________ and come early for
(double consonant **rr**)

the ________________________ stuff! Who knows? You might
(consonant blend **st**)

________________________ something you have always wanted! We will
(ends with **er**)

also have a pile of ________________________ stuff that you can just take.
(double vowel **ee**)

It's cold that early, so we give you a ________________________
(consonant blend **fr**)

hot drink with your ________________________.
(silent **e**)

Sale Riddles

Write the spelling word to solve the rhyming riddle.

1. I start with a blend; I rhyme with "spoof." A receipt can be used to show _________________.

2. My soft **c** sound is the last thing you hear. Stores with good _________________ get a big cheer!

3. I start with a blend; I rhyme with "glee." People are happy to get things for _________________.

4. I end with an **n** and start with a **p**. A fact is something that's been _________________ to me.

5. I end with a blend; I rhyme with "vest." Getting something on sale is the _________________!

6. My **y** sounds like a long **e**. I help if something breaks. I'm a _________________.

7. I end with a blend; I rhyme with "lift." A box with a bow is probably a _________________.

8. I end with the first sound in **ring**. When you _________________, you learn something.

best
discover
free
gift
proof
proven
service
warranty

Name _______________

Sale Signs

Read the signs. Some of the words have missing letters. Cut out the letters to finish spelling the words. Then look at how the two words in each row are spelled and write how they are the same.

fr [glue]

glue [esh!]

How are they the same?

____

____

____

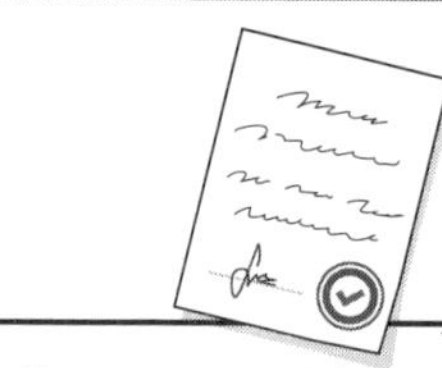

Not many left!

Hu [glue] y!

Comes with a lifetime

warran [glue]

How are they the same?

____

____

____

This is p [glue] fect

for school!

p [glue] chase!

How are they the same?

____

____

____

| ty | er | ee | rr | fr | ur |

Spelling Games and Activities • EMC 8273 • © Evan-Moor Corporation

Name _______________________

What's the Price?

Samir's Sports Supplies is having a sale, but they forgot to write the prices! Use the word on the tag and the chart to write a price for each item. If a word has more than one price, add them.

Letters and Sounds	Price
Soft **c** sound	$18.00
Ending blend	$12.00
Long **e** sound at the end	$24.00
Beginning blend	$10.00

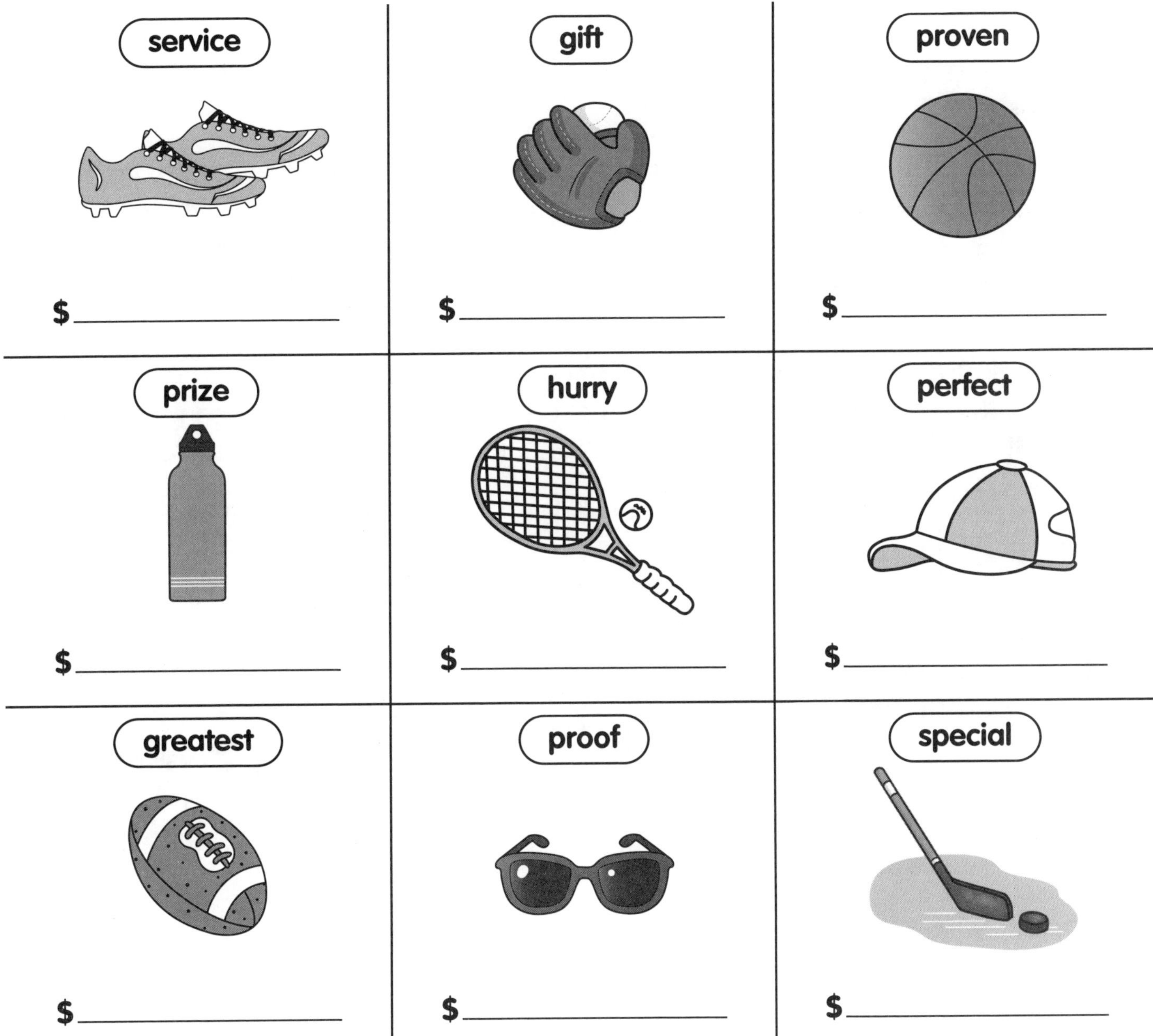

Name ______________________

Sidewalk Sale

Four stores are having a sidewalk sale, but the wind blew their signs away!
Students will put together the torn signs and figure out which store they are from.

What You Need

- Store Cards on this page, cut out
- Sale Signs on pages 29 and 30, cut out

What You Do

1. Print enough copies of the sale signs to give each student one half of a torn sign, making sure that each half of a torn sign has a match. Then make enough copies of the store cards for each pair of students to choose one. Lay out the store cards in one place in the classroom.

2. Distribute one half of a torn sale sign to each student. Explain that these are halves of signs that were torn during a windy sidewalk sale. Say that each whole sign has a spelling word, and they need to find the person who has the other half of their torn sign. Have students find the person who has the other half; this will be their partner.

3. After all students have found the matching half of their torn sign, direct partners to the store cards. Have the partners figure out which store their sign came from and take that card. Tell them there are clues on the cards to help them figure it out.

4. When all the partners have chosen a store, ask each pair to tell which store their sign came from and the clue they used to figure it out.

Sale Signs

Cut out the torn signs. Give each student one half of a torn sign.

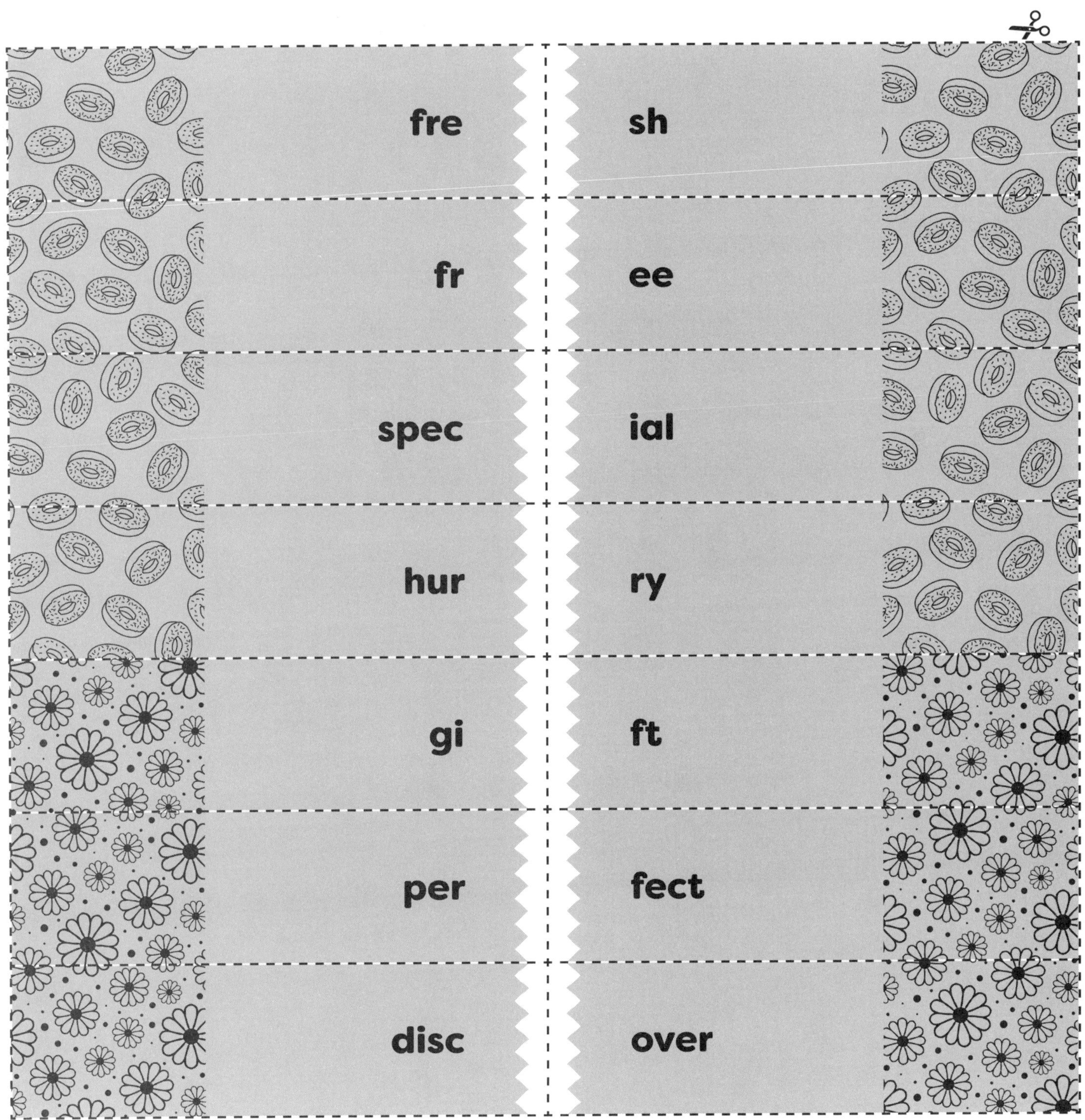

Sale Signs, *continued*

pri	ze
pro	ven
be	st
grea	test
pro	of
war	ranty
ser	vice
purc	hase

WORLD OF SCIENCE

Practice spelling and using these science words that name things from the air, technology, and living things.

- ☐ fog
- ☐ smog
- ☐ frost
- ☐ pollen
- ☐ thermometer
- ☐ telescope
- ☐ element
- ☐ expand

- ☐ magnet
- ☐ habitat
- ☐ animal
- ☐ mammal
- ☐ insect
- ☐ reptile
- ☐ colony

SPELLING TIPS

☆ A vowel between two consonants is usually short. Example: **fin**

☆ A **silent e** after a vowel and consonant usually makes the vowel long. Example: **vine**

☆ Most words with more than one syllable have a **schwa** (ə) sound. There is no rule for which vowel to use to spell it.

Name _______________________

The Way Home

Help the bee find the path to its colony. Color the squares that have
a **short o** sound.

START	insect	pollen	fog	frost
frost	colony	fog	magnet	thermometer
magnet	telescope	expand	habitat	colony
fog	pollen	smog	reptile	smog
colony	insect	frost	fog	thermometer
smog	thermometer	mammal	element	animal
expand	frost	pollen	colony	END

   Spelling Games and Activities • EMC 8273 • © Evan-Moor Corporation

Name _______________________

Discover What's Inside

When you look closely at something, sometimes you'll find a hidden surprise!
Look at the letters in each spelling word. Use them to make other words.
Write them in the shell. The first one is done for you.

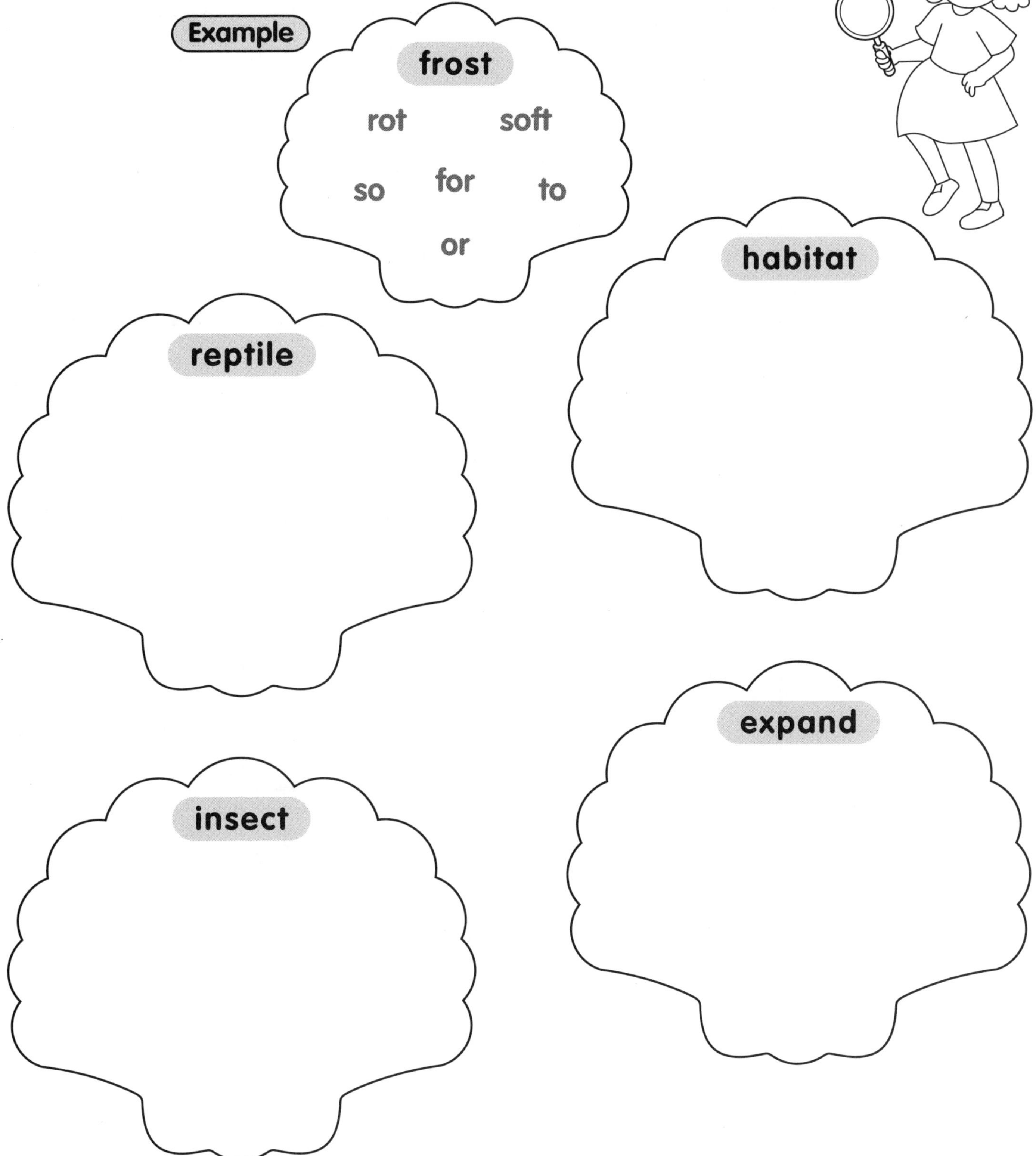

Name ___________________________

Use Your Clues

Look closely at the starting, ending, and vowel sounds of the clue words in the example. They describe a science word in the box. The science word will have the same sounds, but the spelling may be different from the clue words.

> element   expand   ~~fog~~   magnet   mammal   pollen

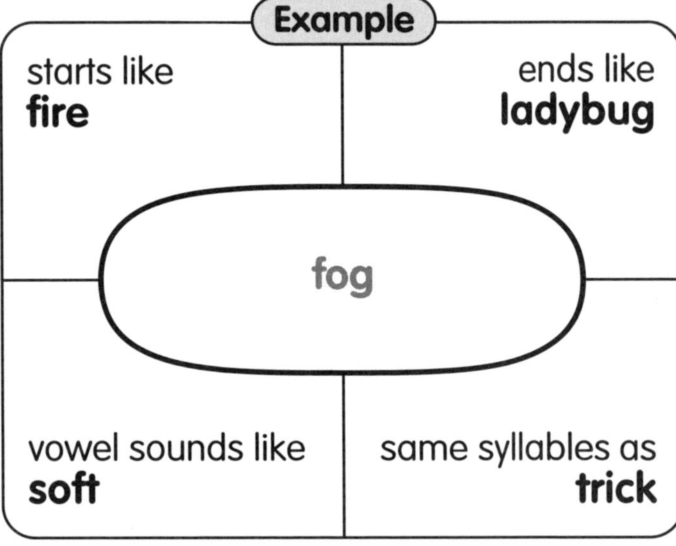

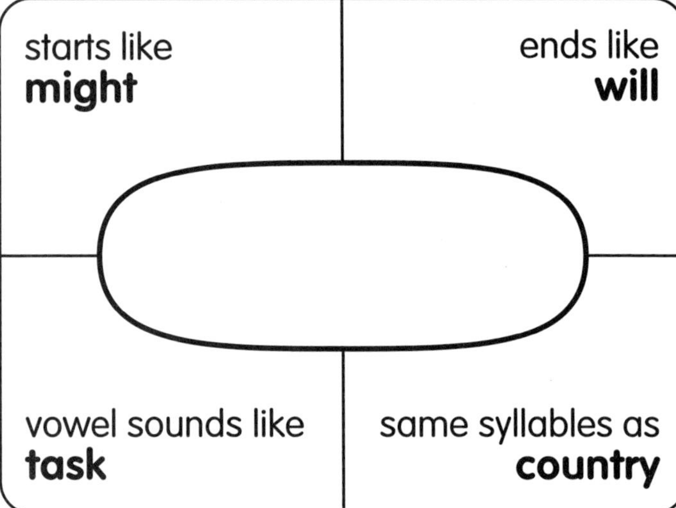

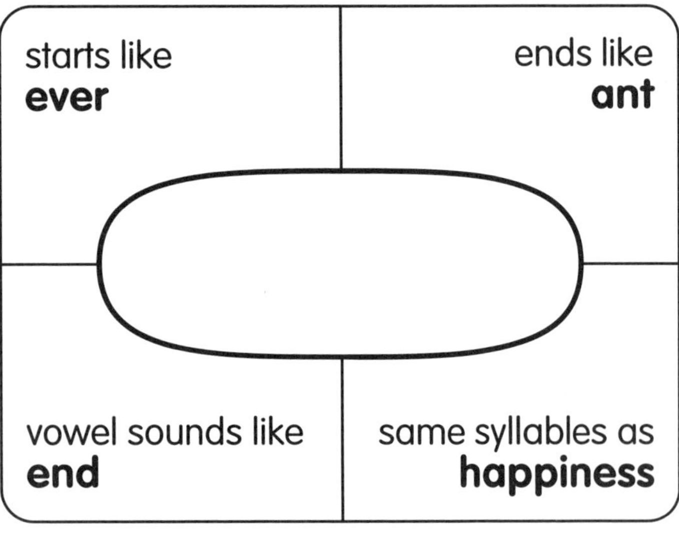

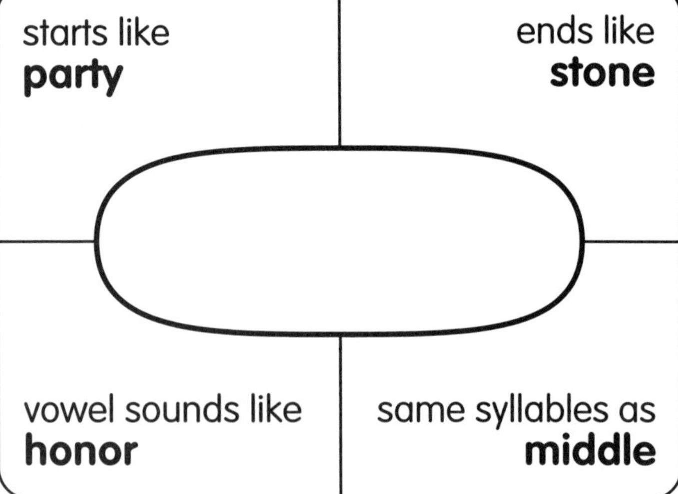

    Spelling Games and Activities • EMC 8273 • © Evan-Moor Corporation

Name _______________________

It's Raining Vowels!

The vowels fell out of the words below! Luckily, it is raining vowels.
Use the letters in the raindrops to finish spelling the words.
Cross off each vowel after you use it.

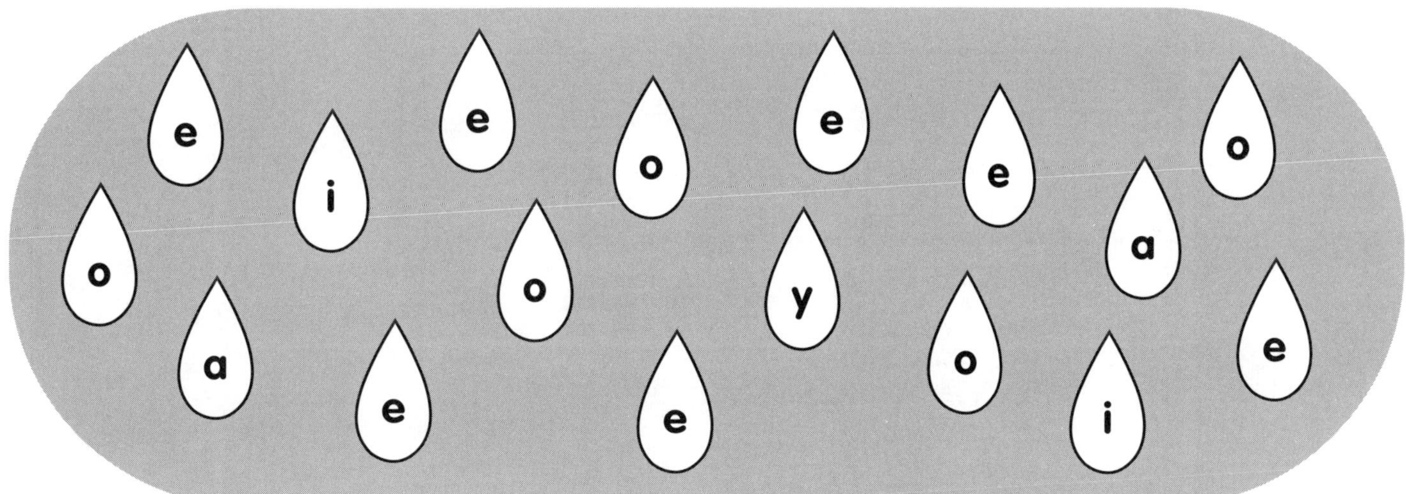

1. s m ___ g

____

2. ___ n ___ m ___ l

____

3. ___ n s ___ c t

____

4. t ___ l ___ s c ___ p ___

____

5. t h ___ r m ___ m ___ t ___ r

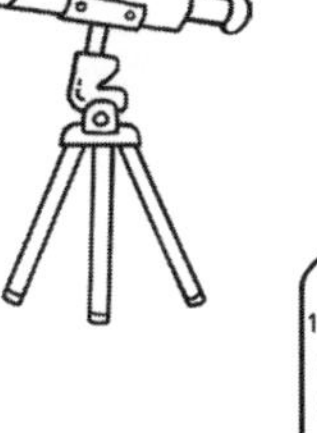

____

6. c ___ l ___ n ___

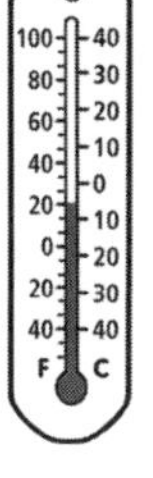

Name _______________________

Changing Words

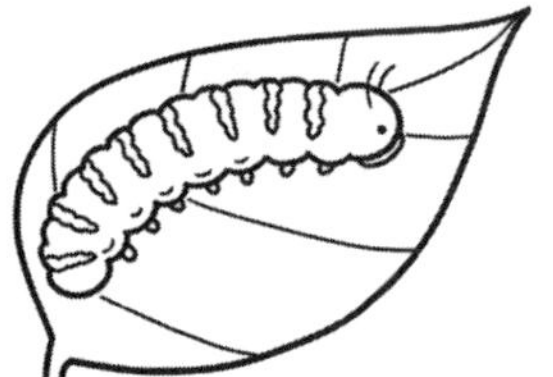

Some animals change how they look during their lives.
You can change the silly phrases below to spell science words.
Unscramble each phrase to write a spelling word on the line.

> animal   element   habitat
> magnet   reptile   telescope

1. lip tree   _______________________

2. get man   _______________________

3. bait hat   _______________________

4. teen elm   _______________________

5. am nail   _______________________

6. let cop see   _______________________

Spelling Games and Activities • EMC 8273 • © Evan-Moor Corporation

Name ______________________

Schwa Zones

Read each word in the box and decide which vowels are making a schwa sound. Circle the vowels. Then write each word in its Schwa Zone. If a word has more than one schwa, write the word in each zone. Use a different color for each zone.

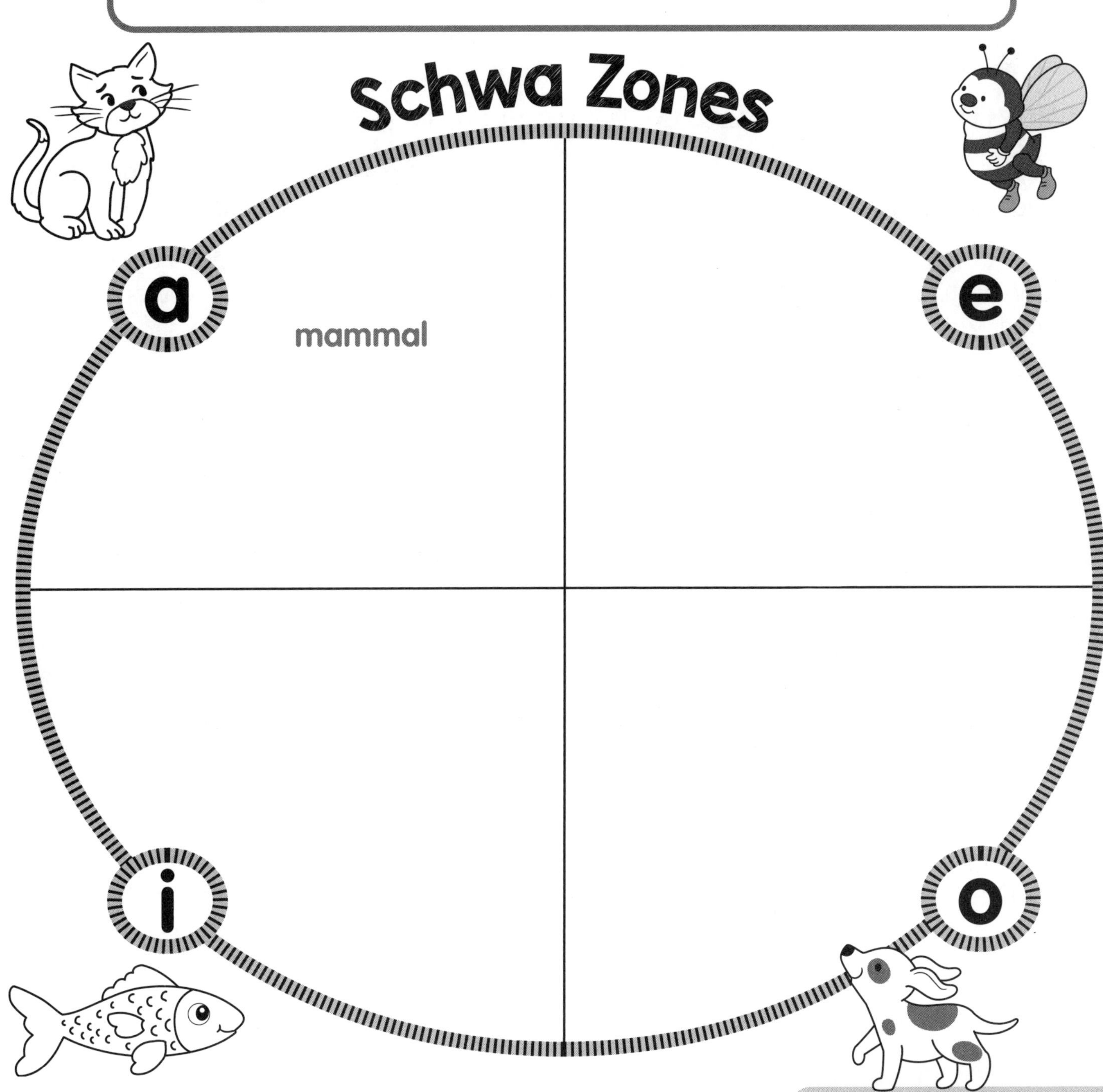

Name ______________________________

Tic-Tac-Type

Students play a familiar game in a new way, with spelling words instead of letters.

What You Need

- Spelling Word List on page 39
- Game Board on page 40
- pencils

How to Play

The object is to get 3 of your words in a line in any direction on a tic-tac-toe board.

1. Put students in pairs. Distribute to each pair 2 spelling word lists and one game board for each game they will play, along with a pencil for each student.

2. Explain to students that players take turns claiming a square as in regular tic-tac-toe. But instead of marking an **X** or an **O** in the square, players write a word from their word type.

3. Assign or have students choose a pair of word types:

   - **technology** words
   - **living things** words
   ____
   - words with a **short a** sound
   - words with a **short o** sound
   ____
   - words with **1 or 2** syllables
   - words with **3 or 4** syllables

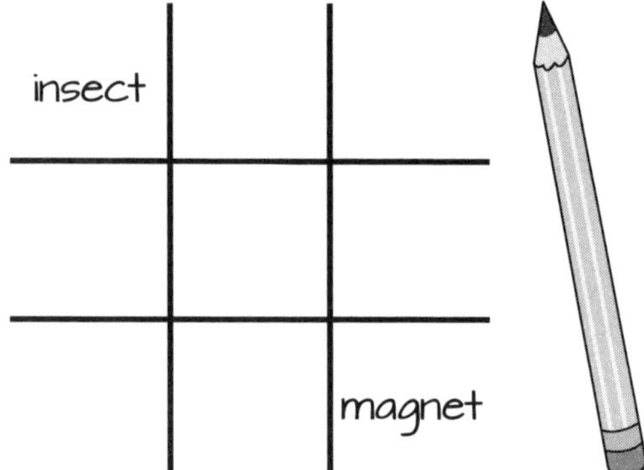

   Have players look at the spelling list and find the words in their word types.

4. The first player writes one of his or her words in a square. It must be spelled correctly to count! Then the second player writes one of his or her words in a different square. Players continue until one has 3 words in a row, either across, up and down, or diagonally. If neither player can make a row of 3 words, the game is a tie. See examples of winning and tie games on the word list sheet.

5. Give students another pair of word types and play again. Players take turns going first in each game played.

          Spelling Games and Activities • EMC 8273 • © Evan-Moor Corporation

Spelling Word List

Use these words to play tic-tac-type:

telescope	fog	animal
element	smog	mammal
expand	frost	insect
magnet	pollen	reptile
thermometer	habitat	colony

Examples of winning games:

Game 1

short a word	short o word	short o word
short a word	short a word	short a word
short o word	short a word	short o word

Game 2

short a word	short o word	short a word
short o word	short a word	
short o word		short a word

Game 3

short a word	short a word	short o word
short a word	short o word	
short o word	short o word	short a word

Examples of tie games:

Game 1

short o word		short a word
short a word	short a word	short o word
short o word	short o word	short a word

Game 2

	short a word	short o word
short o word	short o word	short a word
short a word	short o word	short a word

Game 3

short a word	short o word	short a word
short a word		short o word
short o word	short a word	short o word

Game Board

Name _______________________

Name _______________________

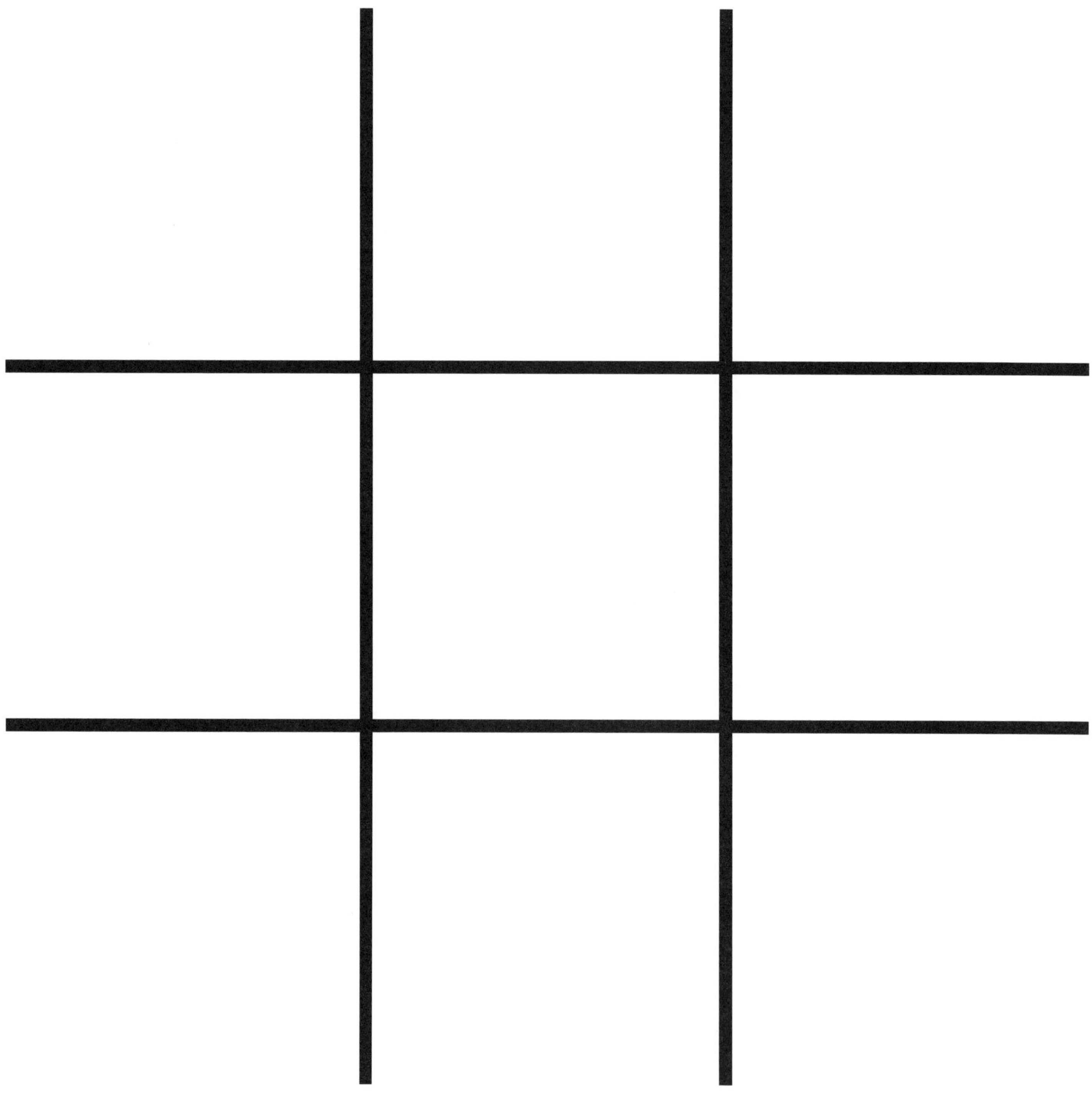

Spelling Games and Activities • EMC 8273 • © Evan-Moor Corporation

READY, SET, GO!

Practice spelling and using these sports words that name different sports, their goals, and the people who play them.

- ☐ soccer
- ☐ tennis
- ☐ pickleball
- ☐ volleyball
- ☐ handball
- ☐ softball
- ☐ baseball
- ☐ teammate
- ☐ opponent
- ☐ winner
- ☐ athlete
- ☐ compete
- ☐ marathon
- ☐ practice
- ☐ fitness

SPELLING TIPS

⭐ Two consonants following a vowel often make the vowel short. Example: **hockey**

⭐ Break up compound words into smaller words to make them easier to say and spell. Example: **football = foot + ball**

⭐ Most words with more than one syllable have a **schwa** sound. There is no rule for which vowel to use to spell it.

Name ___________________

Reach the Goal

The player can kick the ball to words that have a short vowel sound.
Draw the player's path up the soccer field to the goal at the top.

Spelling Games and Activities • EMC 8273 • © Evan-Moor Corporation

Name ___________

E for Effort

Read each word. Decide if each **e** in the word is silent or what kind of sound it has. Use the chart to give points to each **e**. Add them. Write the word's score.

Sound	Points
silent **e**	1
schwa	2
r-controlled **e**	3
short **e**	4
long **e**	5

1. athlete **Score** ____

2. baseball **Score** ____

3. fitness **Score** ____

4. opponent **Score** ____

5. pickleball **Score** ____

6. practice **Score** ____

7. tennis **Score** ____

8. volleyball **Score** ____

9. winner **Score** ____

Name ______________________

Choosing Teams

Cyrus and Calista are choosing teams. Cyrus chooses players with a nickname that has 2 syllables. Calista chooses players with a nickname that has 3 syllables. Draw a line from each player to Cyrus or Calista.

Baseball

Volleyball

Softball

Practice

Marathon

2 syllables

Cyrus

3 syllables

Calista

Pickleball

Handball

Opponent

Teammate

Soccer

Name _______________________

First Place

What did the winners receive? Read the word in each space.
Color each space following these rules:

- Use orange for words that have a **long vowel** sound.
- Use green for words that have a **short vowel** sound AND are **compound**.
- Use yellow for words that have a **short vowel** sound but are **NOT compound**.

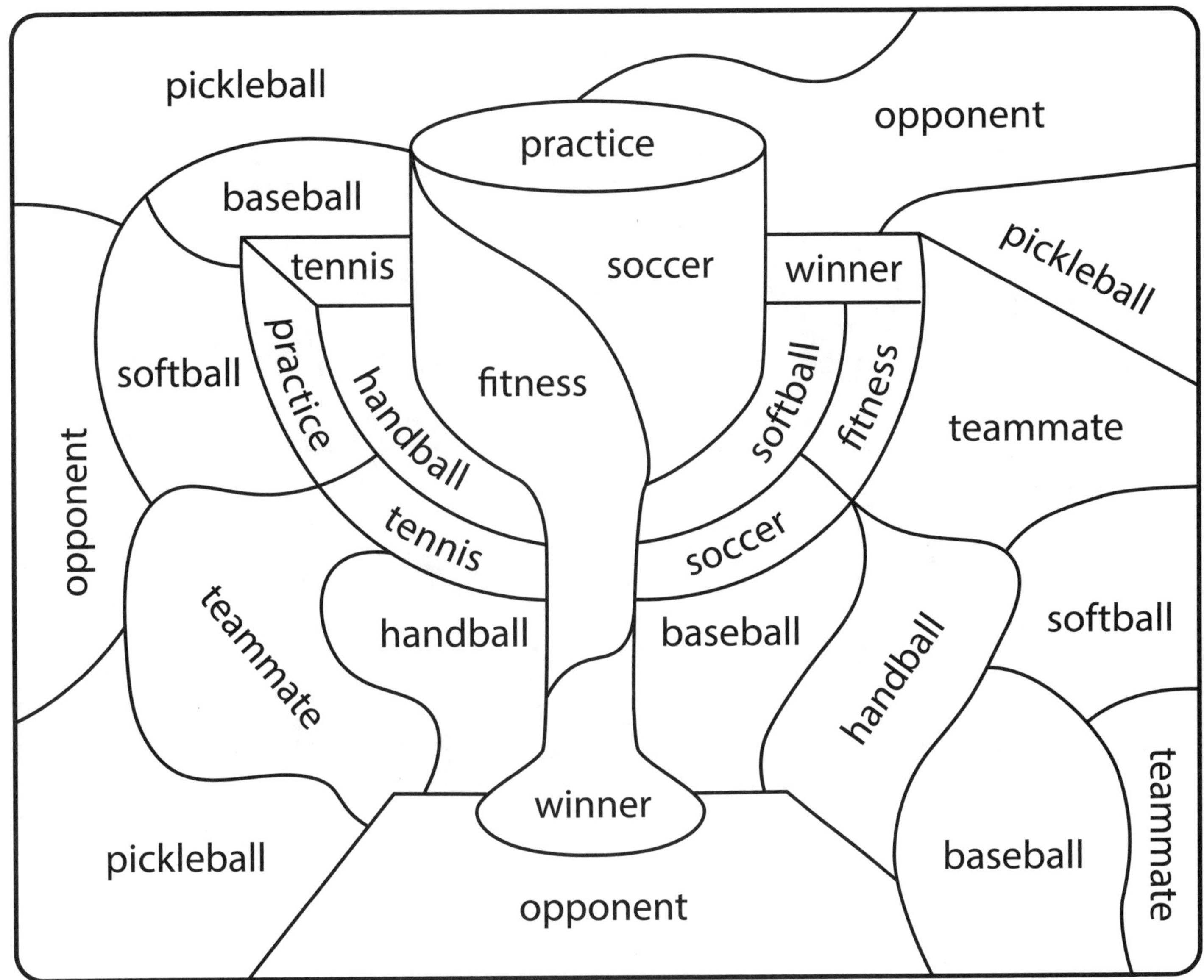

Name _______________________

Word Relay

In a relay race, teammates work together. One starts the race, and the other finishes it. These two teammates have run a lot of word races. Cut out each part of a race. Match them to finish a race. Glue them onto pages 47 and 48 and write the words.

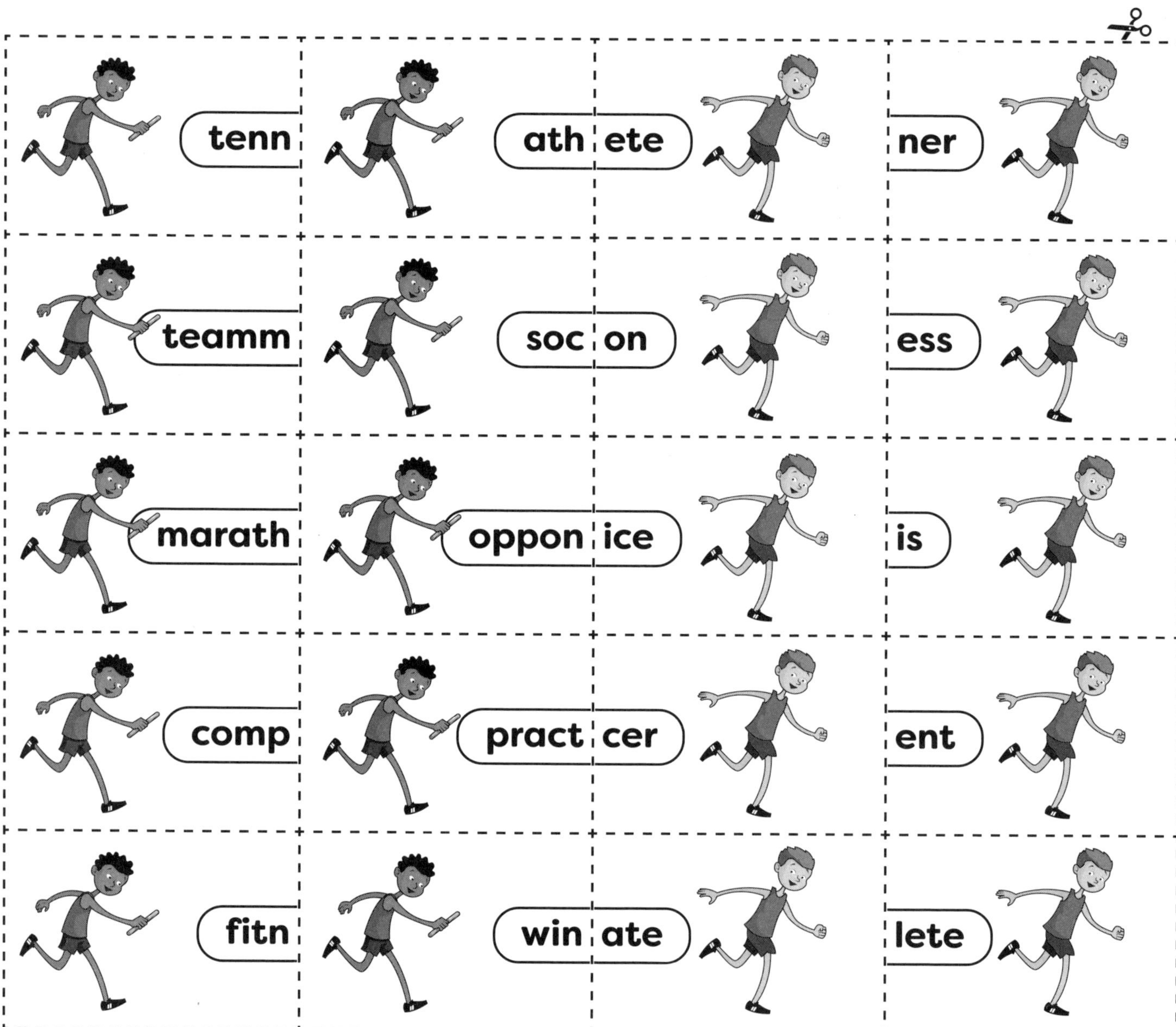

Spelling Games and Activities • EMC 8273 • © Evan-Moor Corporation

Word Relay, *continued*

Glue together each pair of runners who make a spelling word and write their word on the Finish Line.

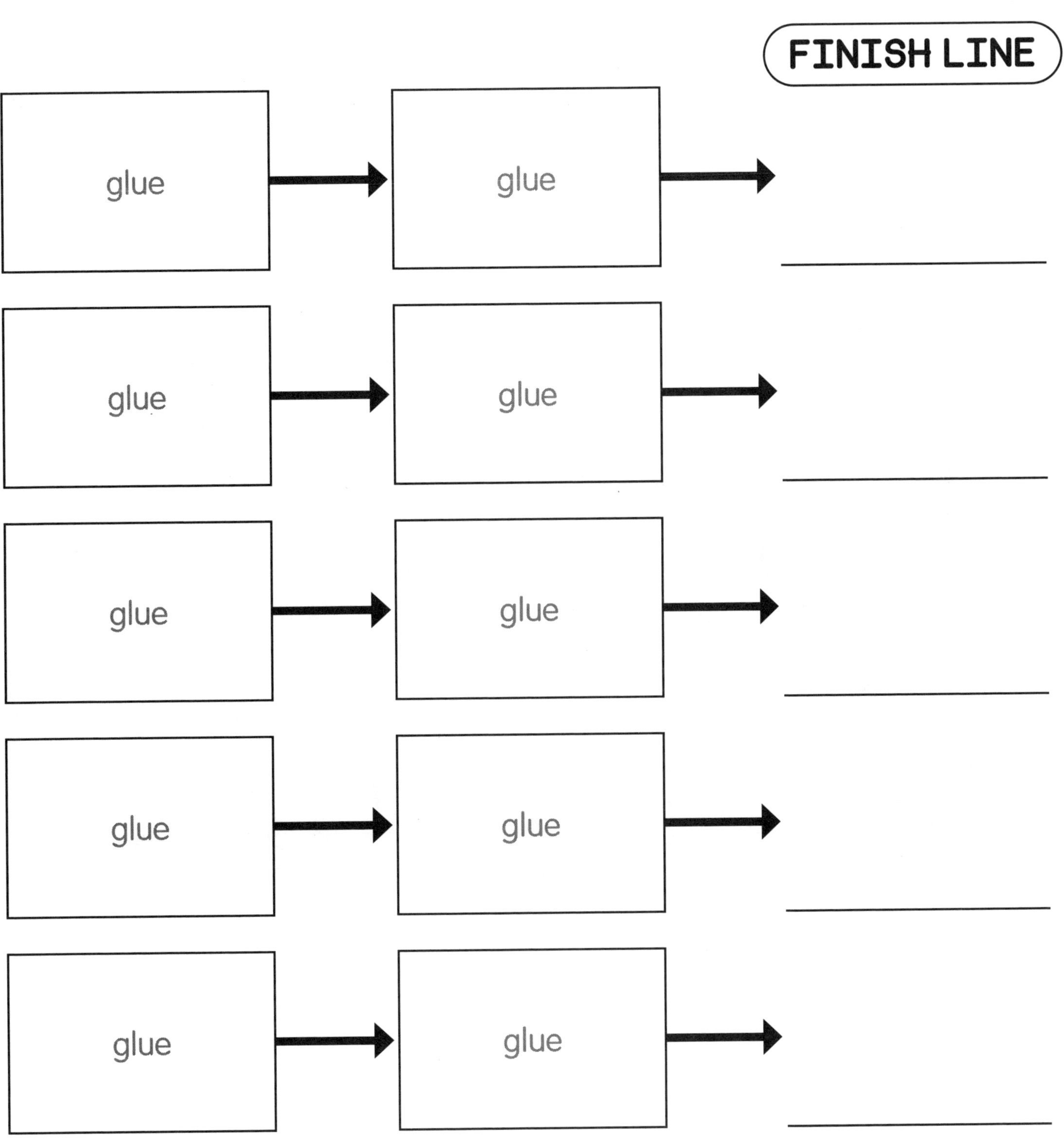

Name _______________________

Word Relay, *continued*

Glue together each pair of runners who make a spelling word and write their word on the Finish Line.

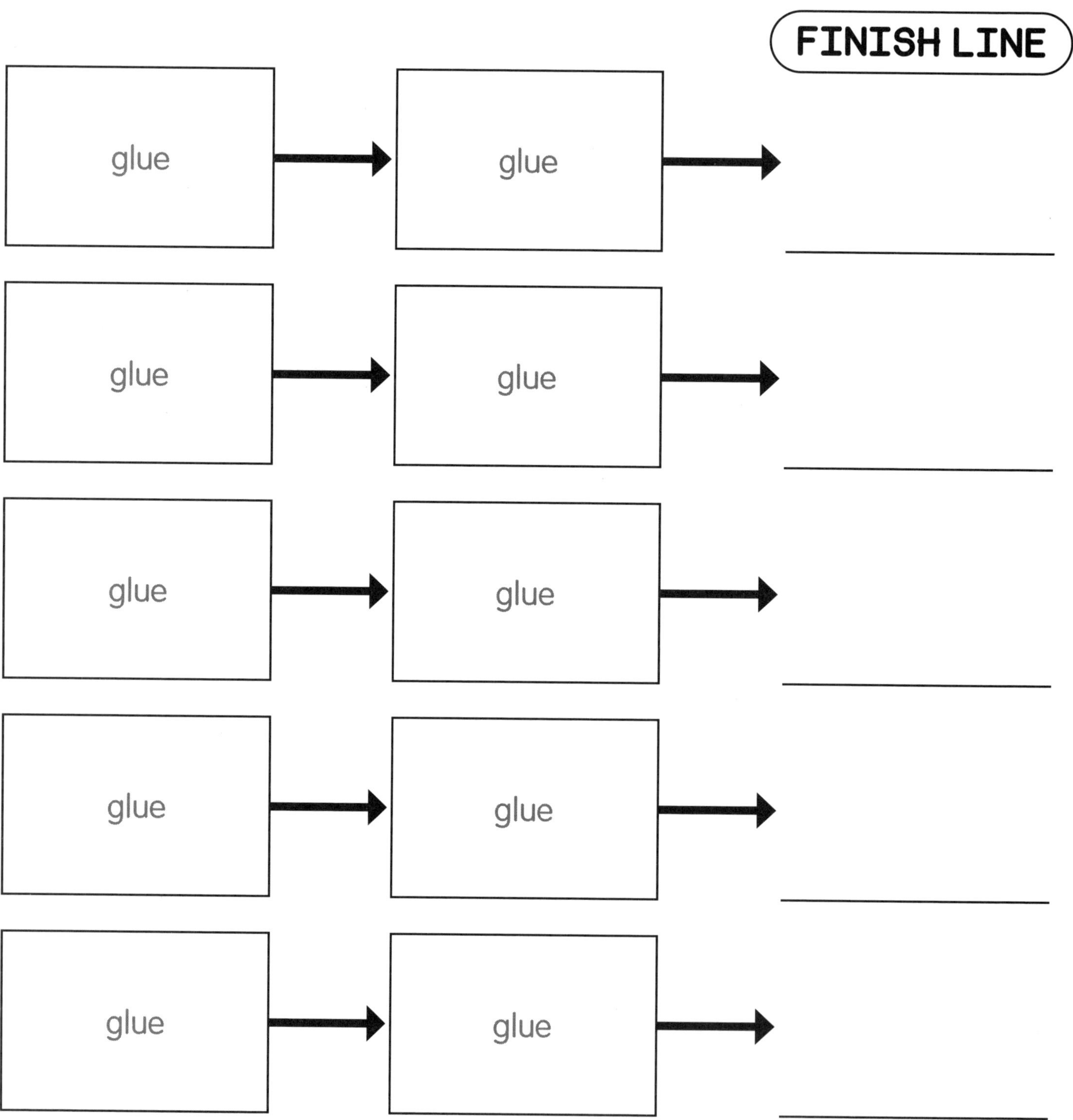

Spelling Games and Activities • EMC 8273 • © Evan-Moor Corporation

Name ________________

Dunk a Word

Teams spell words and toss them into a wastebasket for points.

What You Need

- Ready, Set, Go! spelling word list on page 41
- Goal Labels on page 50
- 2 clean, empty wastebaskets, boxes, or similar containers (each team's goal)
- throw-line markers
- 15 sheets of blank paper, cut into quarters
- markers or crayons

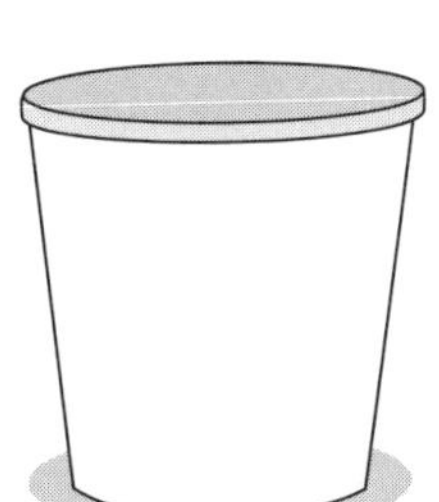

How to Play

The object of the game is to toss correctly spelled words into a basket.

1. Divide the class into 2 teams. Distribute 3 quarter sheets of paper and a marker or crayon to each player. Place each goal about 6 feet (1.8 meters) from a throw-line marker. The throwing areas should be far enough apart so that the teams won't be in each other's way when throwing. Attach each team's goal label to its goal.

2. Have each team line up behind its throw line. The teacher calls out a spelling word. The first two players on each team write the word on their first sheet of paper, wad it into a ball, and toss it into their team's goal.

3. Continue with the remaining spelling words, rotating players on each team so that all players get to spell several words.

4. When all paper balls have been tossed, the teacher collects them from the first goal and unfolds them (players can help). Sort the papers by word. Then show the players each of the papers for each word and have them identify which are spelled correctly. Each correct paper is worth 1 point. Repeat with the other team's goal. The team with the most points wins!

   The game can also be played by folding each word paper into a paper airplane.

Goal Labels

SPACE ADVENTURE

Practice spelling and using these space and technology words that name things you would take to and see in space.

- ☐ galaxy
- ☐ orbit
- ☐ asteroid
- ☐ planet
- ☐ exploration
- ☐ spaceship
- ☐ spacesuit
- ☐ robot

- ☐ machine
- ☐ invention
- ☐ transportation
- ☐ deploy
- ☐ journey
- ☐ rocket
- ☐ universe

SPELLING TIPS

- ★ The letter **y** is sometimes a vowel that has a **long e** sound. It is also used in the diphthong **oy**. Examples: **sunny, toy**
- ★ The letters **-tion** are a suffix. It sounds like **shun**. Example: **action**
- ★ Break up compound words into smaller words to make them easier to say and spell. Example: **moonlight = moon + light**

Name _______________

Missing in Space

Some letters floated out of the space words! Use the letters to finish spelling each word. Cross off each letter after you use it.

| deploy | galaxy | journey | machine | orbit | planet | robot | rocket |

a	a	a	b	c	c	e	e	e
g	i	i	l	l	n	n	o	o
o	o	r	t	t	u	y	y	y

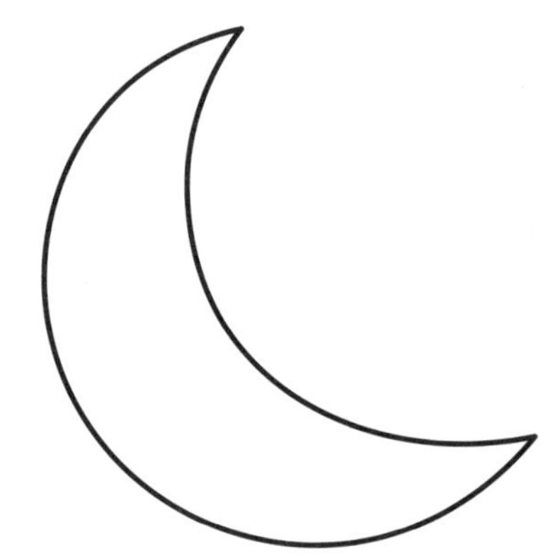

1. ___ a ___ ___ ___ x ___

2. pl___ ___ e ___

3. j___ ___ r ___ e ___

4. r___ ___ k ___ t

5. d___ p ___ o ___

6. ___ r ___ ___ t

7. ___ ob ___ ___

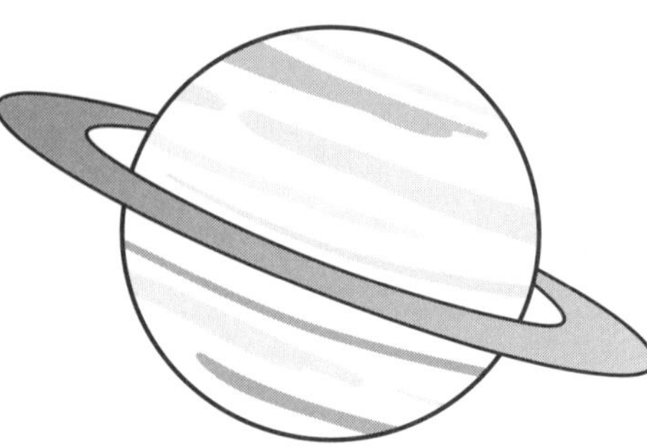

8. m___ ___ h ___ n ___

Spelling Games and Activities • EMC 8273 • © Evan-Moor Corporation

Name _______________

Space Word Riddles

Read the clue. Write a spelling word to solve the riddle.

asteroid	deploy	transportation
universe	planet	spacesuit
invention	orbit	spaceship

1. I rhyme with the name **Janet**.

____

2. I start with a conjunction. 

____

3. My last four letters rhyme with **toy**. 

____

4. I am a compound word, but you don't wear me.

____

5. My suffix is **-tion**, and I am something new. 

____

6. I have four syllables and **port** in the middle. 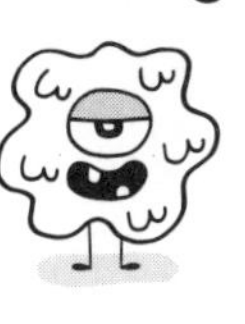

____

7. I fly through space, and I end with **oid**. 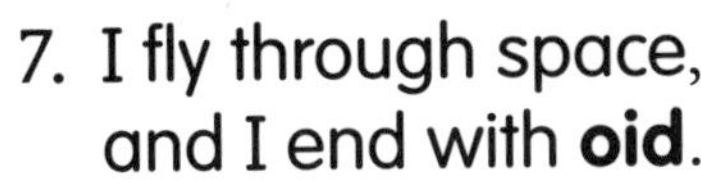

____

8. I have a **soft c**, and you wear me. 

____

9. I start with a long vowel and end with a **silent e**. 

____

Rhymes in Space

Name ______________________

Write the spelling word that the rhyming clue describes.

asteroid	exploration	invention	journey	orbit
planet	robot	spaceship	transportation	universe

1. My path goes around like the shape of a crown.

   ______________________ (ends in **t**)

2. I'm something new made by you.

   ______________________ (has a **v**)

3. If you dare, we'll go from here to there.

   ______________________ (begins with a **j**)

4. Use your mind to see what you can find.

   ______________________ (has an **x**)

5. When seen from afar, I look like a star.

   ______________________ (ends in **t**)

6. When I make a crater, you'll still see it years later.

   ______________________ (has **er**)

7. I am programmed to do things just like you.

   ______________________ (has a **long o** sound)

8. I fly through the sky in a race to space.

   ______________________ (compound word)

9. I can be a train or a boat or a plane.

   ______________________ (has 3 of the letter **t**)

10. No matter how long you spend, you'll never reach my end.

    ______________________ (ends in an **s** sound)

Name _______________

Lost in Space

Follow the directions to help the astronauts get to their spaceships.

Read each word out loud. Color the squares of the words that have a consonant blend.

START →

asteroid	universe	invention
galaxy	planet	transportation	orbit
universe	robot	spacesuit	galaxy
machine	journey	deploy	exploration

END 

Read each word out loud. Color the squares of the 3-syllable words and the 4-syllable words.

START ↓

orbit	journey	robot
universe	rocket	planet	spaceship
galaxy	transportation	spacesuit	deploy
machine	exploration	asteroid	invention

END

Space Puzzle

Cut apart the puzzle pieces. Use them to complete page 57.

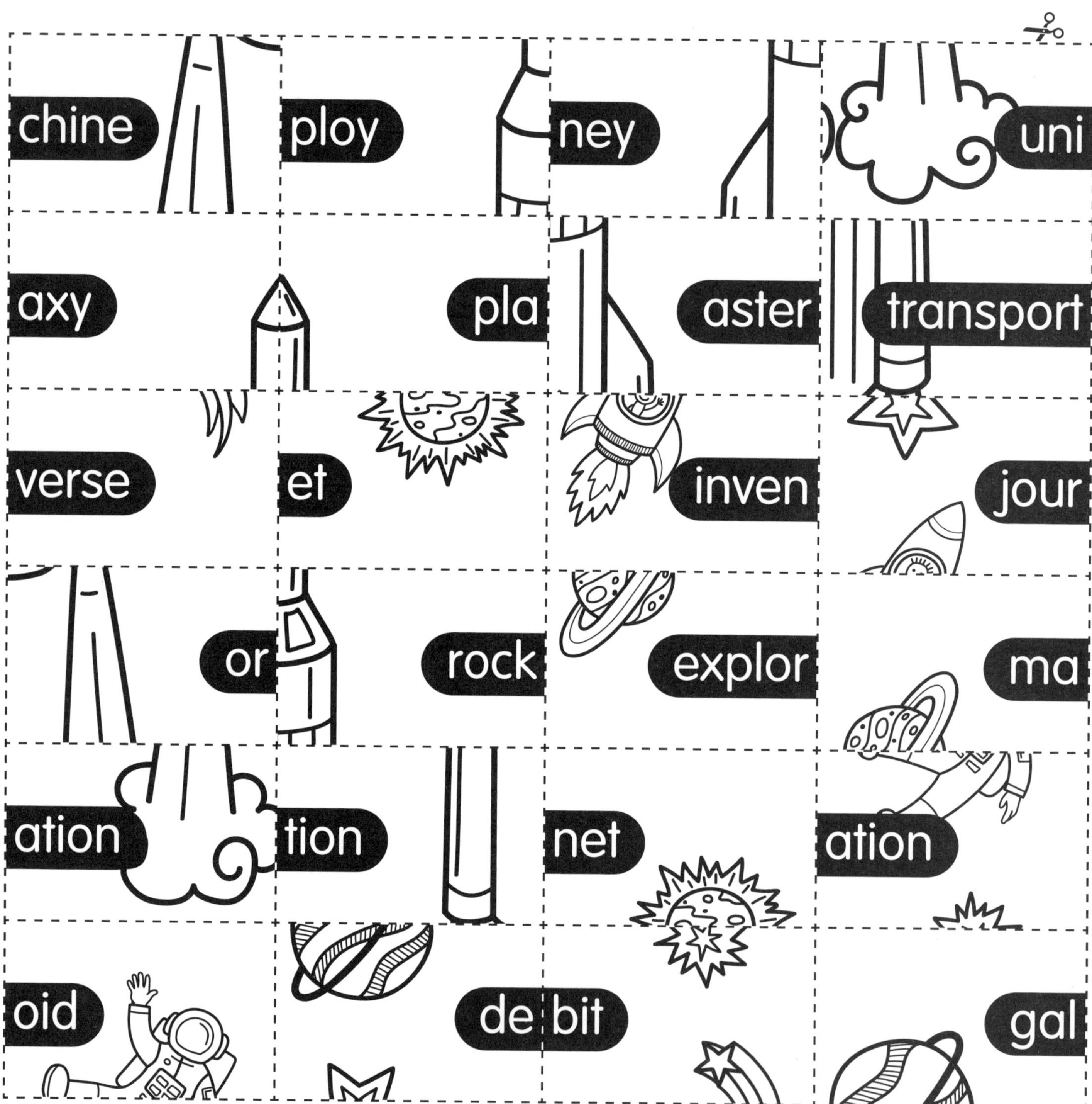

Spelling Games and Activities • EMC 8273 • © Evan-Moor Corporation

Name _______________________

Space Puzzle, *continued*

Put the puzzle pieces together to make words. Then move them to make a picture of a rocket. Glue them together below.

glue	glue	glue	glue
glue	glue	glue	glue
glue	glue	glue	glue
glue	glue	glue	glue
glue	glue	glue	glue
glue	glue	glue	glue

Name _______________________

I'll Spell It!

Students listen to clues to guess a word and spell it.

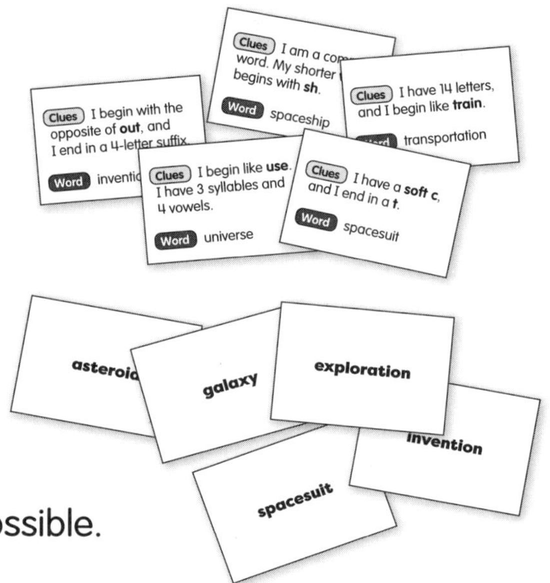

What You Need

- Clues on page 59
- Word Cards on page 60

How to Play

The object of the game is to spell as many words as possible.

1. Print one copy of the clues and cut them apart. Print copies of the word cards (one sheet for every 5 students) and cut them apart.

2. Distribute 3 word cards to each student. Have them read their words silently.

3. Explain to students that you will read clues about a word, and students will look at their word cards to see if they have the word that fits the clues.

   - If a student has the word, he or she shouts, "I'll spell it!" The student places the card facedown and spells the word out loud. If the spelling is correct, you shout, "You spelled it!" If the spelling is incorrect, let the student know.

   - Give other students who have the same card and who shout, "I'll spell it!" an opportunity to spell the word.

4. Continue with the next clue, giving each student who shouts, "I'll spell it!" an opportunity to spell the word that matches. The game ends when all clues are used.

Spelling Games and Activities • EMC 8273 • © Evan-Moor Corporation

Clues

Clues I begin like **jog**, and I have 3 vowels.

Word journey

Clues I include the word **ax**. My last letter has a **long e** sound.

Word galaxy

Clues You hear **long o** and **short o** sounds. I have 5 letters.

Word robot

Clues I begin with the opposite of **out**, and I end in a 4-letter suffix.

Word invention

Clues I begin like **use**. I have 3 syllables and 4 vowels.

Word universe

Clues I begin with a consonant blend, and I include **net**.

Word planet

Clues I begin with **a** and end with **d**. I have 8 letters.

Word asteroid

Clues I start with a vowel, and I have a **short i**.

Word orbit

Clues I have **ch** in my middle, and it sounds like **sh**.

Word machine

Clues I have a **soft c**, and I end in a **t**.

Word spacesuit

Clues I have a consonant blend in my middle. I end in **oy**.

Word deploy

Clues I have a **hard c**, and I end in a **t**.

Word rocket

Clues I am a compound word. My shorter word begins with **sh**.

Word spaceship

Clues You hear **x** at my beginning and see **tion** at my end.

Word exploration

Clues I have 14 letters, and I begin like **train**.

Word transportation

Word Cards

galaxy	robot	exploration
transportation	deploy	journey
rocket	universe	invention
orbit	machine	spaceship
asteroid	planet	spacesuit

WHERE TO?

Practice spelling and using these travel words that name ways to travel, where to go, and things to do.

- ☐ voyage
- ☐ passenger
- ☐ cruise
- ☐ roam
- ☐ leisure
- ☐ airline
- ☐ overseas
- ☐ road trip

- ☐ coastline
- ☐ sightseeing
- ☐ station
- ☐ nation
- ☐ location
- ☐ elevation
- ☐ relaxation

SPELLING TIPS

☆ Vowel digraphs **oa**, **ea**, **ei**, and **ui** often have the sound of their first letter. Examples: railr**oa**d, s**ea**, l**ei**sure, s**ui**tcase

☆ Break up compound words into smaller words to make them easier to say and spell. Example: **seashell = sea + shell**

☆ Some compound words are written as two words.

☆ The letters -**tion** are a suffix. It sounds like **shun**. Example: **vacation**

Name ______________________

Bus Ride

Look at the map of the city bus stops. Joy is going to the Roam Hotel. The bus she takes goes to every stop with a long vowel in its name. Draw a line from Joy to each stop her bus will make.

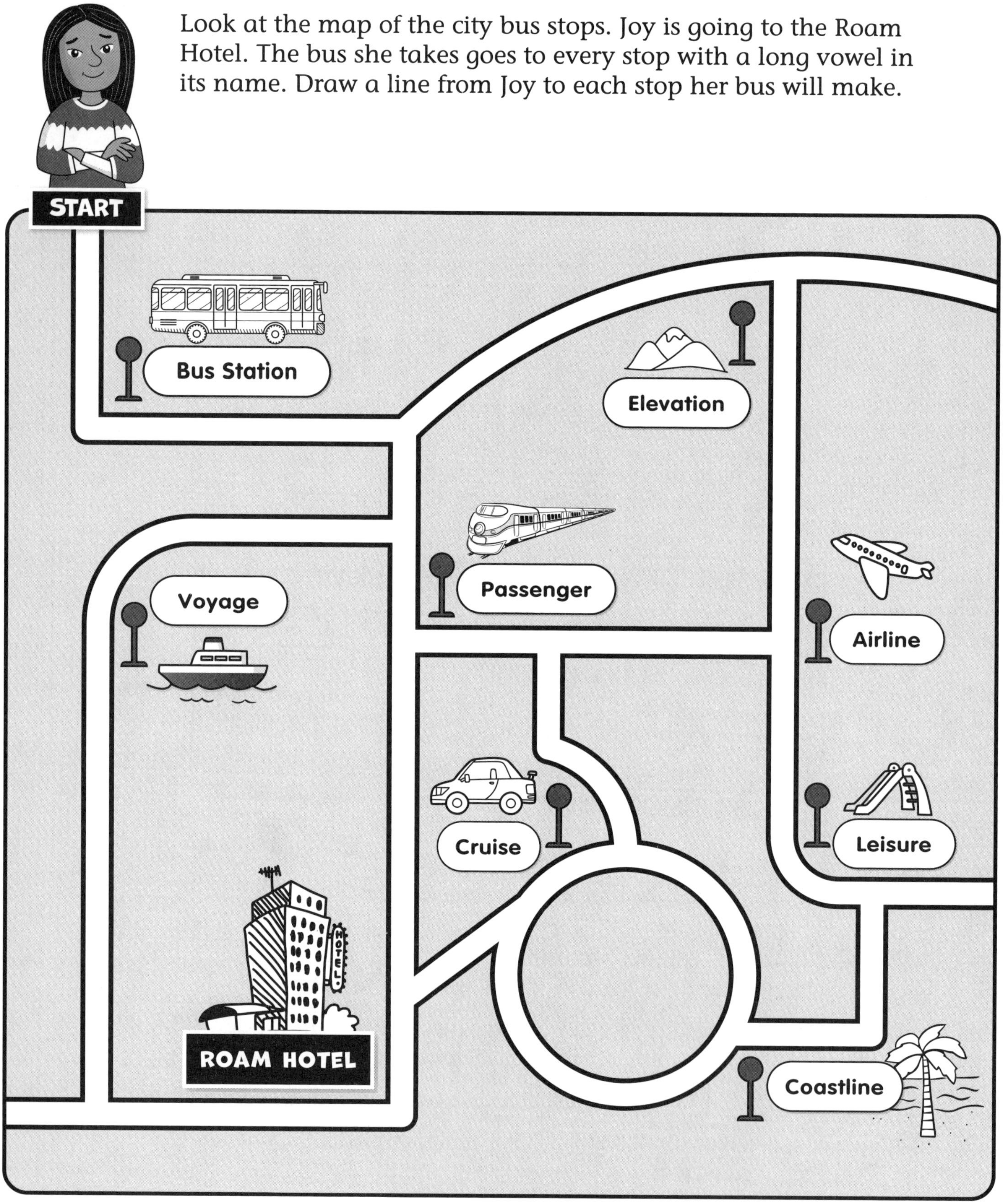

Spelling Games and Activities • EMC 8273 • © Evan-Moor Corporation

Making Connections

Many words can be made from smaller words. Use the words in the box to make as many compound words as you can. Write them below.

air	bee	brush	bus	coast	coat
cook	guide	head	hear	heat	line
mail	over	pass	pay	pipe	port
seas	see	sight	sky	time	tour

Name ______________________

Travel Riddle

One word in each group below is spelled incorrectly. Find the word and spell it correctly in the spaces below the group. Then write the numbered letters in the matching spaces of the riddle to answer it.

Which state helps you write?

___ ___ ___ ___ ___ ___ ___ ___ ___ ___ ___ ___
1   2   3   4   5   6   7   8   9   10   11   12

1. coastline, overseas, passenjer

___ ___ ___ ___ ___ ___ ___ ___ ___
 1   3

2. leesure, airline, station

___ ___ ___ ___ ___ ___ ___
      5

3. nation, voyege, cruise

___ ___ ___ ___ ___ ___
   6

4. costline, road trip, passenger

___ ___ ___ ___ ___ ___ ___ ___ ___
       7   4

5. sightseeing, elivation, passenger

___ ___ ___ ___ ___ ___ ___ ___ ___
  2 8

6. station, airlion, leisure

___ ___ ___ ___ ___ ___ ___
 9   11

7. airline, overseas, staytion

___ ___ ___ ___ ___ ___ ___
  12   10

Moving Goods

Read the word in each space. Color each space following these rules:

- Use blue for **compound** words.
- Use gray for words with a **suffix**.
- Use red for all other words.

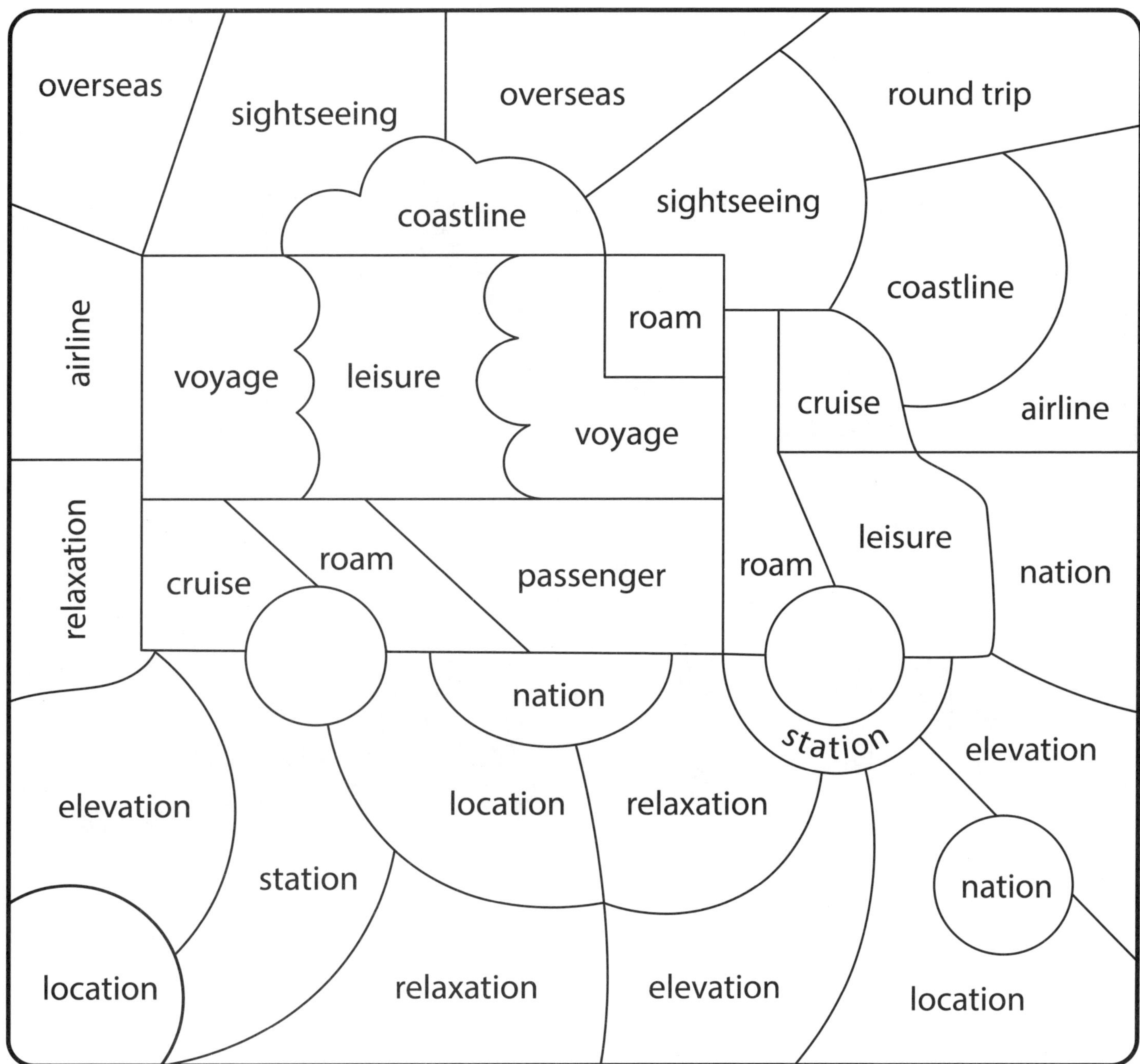

Name _______________________

Our Vacation in Brazil

The Patel family took many photos on vacation. They are writing about each photo.
Some words are missing vowel digraphs. Use the letters on the suitcases to finish
spelling the words. Cross off each vowel after you use it.

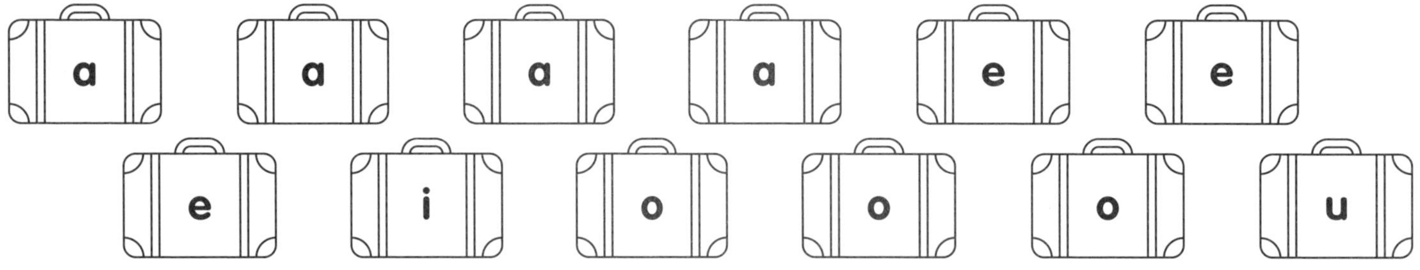

We flew overs _____ _____ s

on R _____ _____ m Air.

I see the c _____ _____ stline from

the window on the plane.

We went sights _____ _____ ing

on a r _____ _____ d trip.

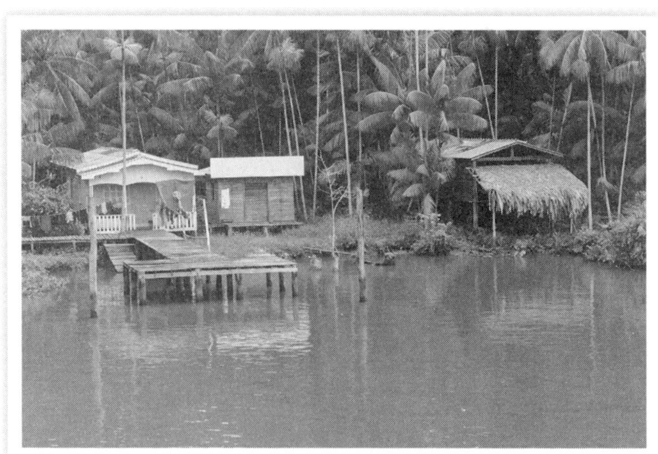

Our cr _____ _____ se sailed down

the Amazon River.

   Spelling Games and Activities • EMC 8273 • © Evan-Moor Corporation

Name ______________________

Roll a Trip

Students spell words correctly to see interesting places around the world.

What You Need

- Spelling Cards from pages 68 and 69 (copied back-to-back and cut out)
- World Game Board on page 70
- die for each group
- game piece for each player

How to Play

The object of the game is to collect as many cards as possible before reaching the end of the trip.

1. Put students in groups of 4 players. Choose one player in each group to be the Card Reader.

2. Distribute a World Game Board and a set of Spelling Cards to each group, along with a die and 4 game pieces. Have the Card Reader place the cards facedown in a stack. Have the other 3 players in the group put their game piece on the START AND END space.

3. Explain to students that on each turn, a player rolls the die and moves the same number of spaces.

   - The Card Reader takes a card from the stack and reads the spelling word out loud.
   - The player spells the word.
     - If it is correct, the player gets the card and looks at the photo to "visit" the place.
     - If the spelling is incorrect, the Card Reader keeps the card.

4. Play continues with the next player. If players run out of cards before all players reach the end, the Card Reader can mix up any used cards that he or she has and continue the game.

5. When all cards have been played and spelled correctly, players count their cards to see who visited the most places. That person switches places with the Card Reader to play the game again.

Spelling Cards (front)

airline	coastline	cruise
elevation	leisure	location
nation	overseas	passenger
relaxation	road trip	roam
sightseeing	station	voyage

Spelling Cards (back)

whale watching

California coastline

flying above clouds

up at the Arctic Circle

amusement park

Swiss Alps

San Francisco cable car

places across the ocean

world's tiniest nation

sheep in Nepal

driving through Spain

relaxing

rocket to outer space

Turkish subway station

tour boat in France

World Game Board

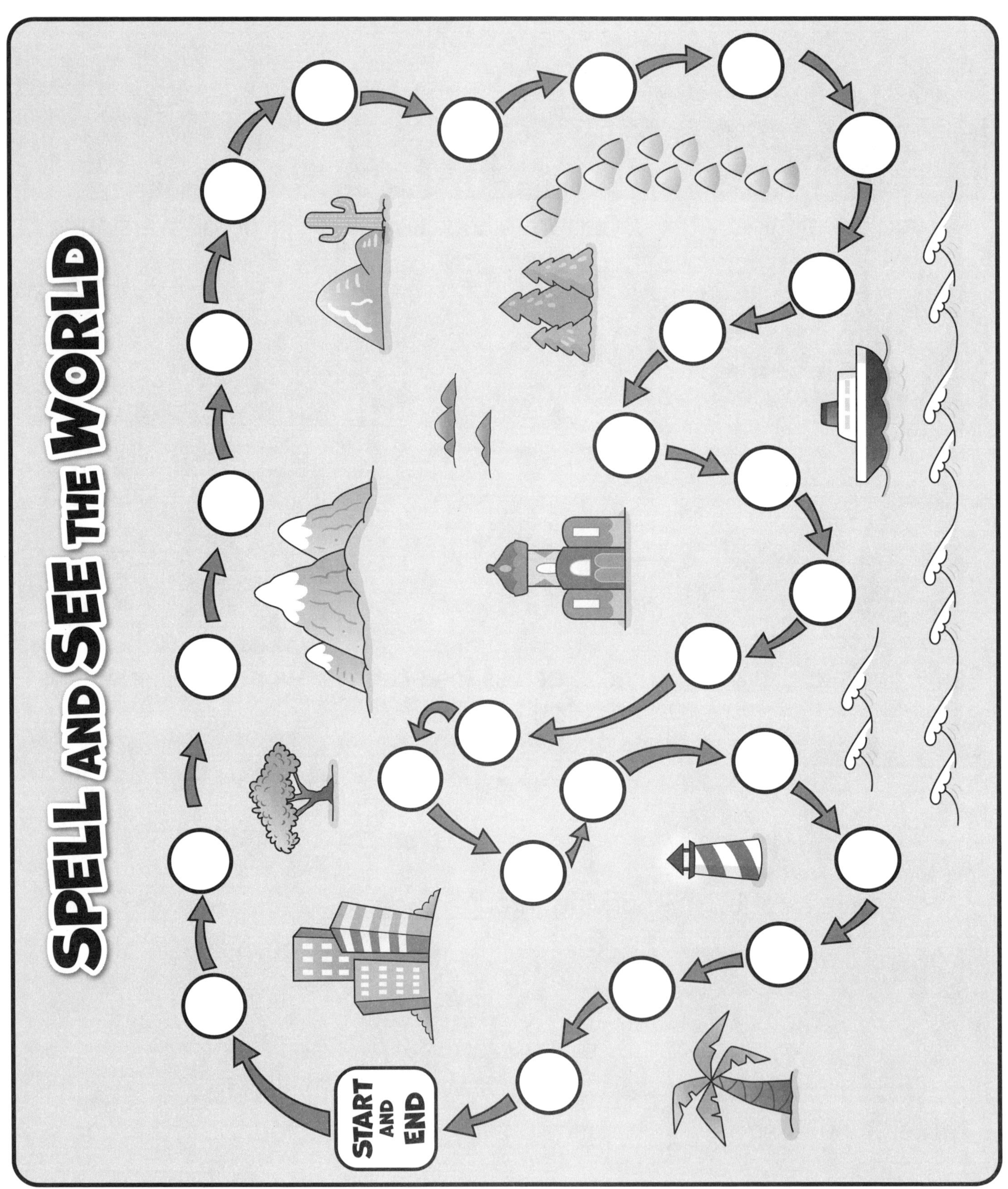

Spelling Games and Activities • EMC 8273 • © Evan-Moor Corporation

MUSIC TO MY EARS

Practice spelling and using these music words that name people who make music, different types of music, and parts of music.

- ☐ melody
- ☐ harmony
- ☐ symphony
- ☐ lullaby
- ☐ chord
- ☐ chorus
- ☐ choir
- ☐ composer
- ☐ conductor
- ☐ performer
- ☐ songwriter
- ☐ recital
- ☐ rehearsal
- ☐ musical
- ☐ bugle

SPELLING TIPS

⭐ **Ch** can make a **hard c** sound in some words. Example: **orchestra**

⭐ A **y** in the middle of a word can have a **short i** sound.
At the end of a word, it has a **long e** or a **long i** sound.
Examples: **melody, lullaby**

⭐ Most words with more than one syllable have a **schwa** sound.
There is no rule for which vowel to use to spell it.

Name _______________

Keeping the Band Together

Read the word in each space. Color each space following these rules:

- Use yellow for words ending in an **l** sound.
- Use red for words starting with a **hard c** sound.
- Use green for words ending in a **long e** or **long i** sound.

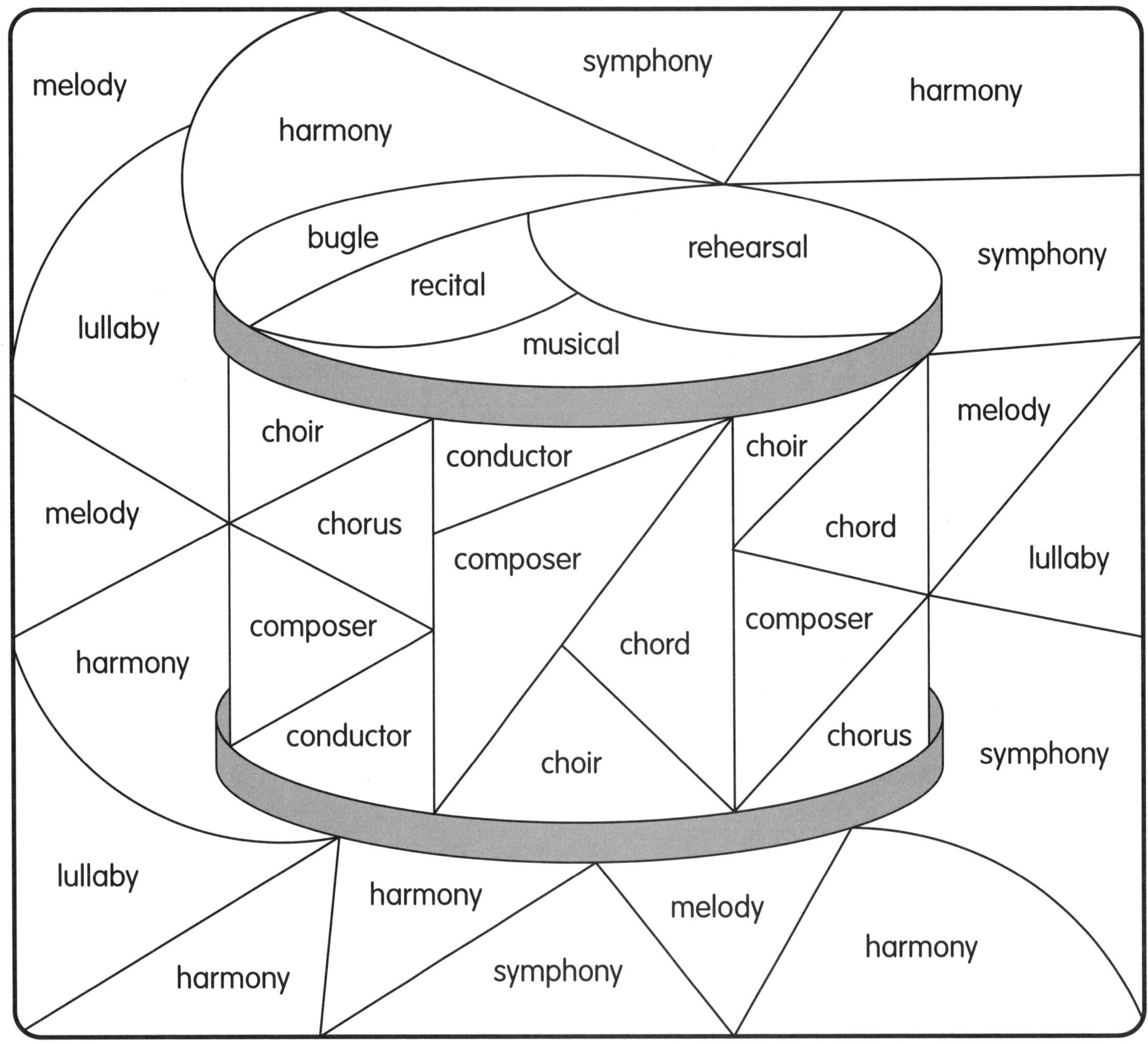

Name _______________________

Hitting Different Notes

The words in each group have something in common, but one of them looks or sounds different. Say each spelling word out loud. Then look at the letters in each word. Find the difference and answer the questions.

1. (**performer**   **conductor**   **songwriter**)

   How do these words **sound** alike? _______________________

   Which one **looks** different? _______________________

   How is it different? _______________________

2. (**melody**   **lullaby**   **symphony**)

   How do these words **look** alike? _______________________

   Which one **sounds** different? _______________________

   How is it different? _______________________

3. (**composer**   **chord**   **choir**)

   How do these words **sound** alike? _______________________

   Which one **looks** different? _______________________

   How is it different? _______________________

Name ___________________________

A Musical Code

Use the code of music notes and symbols to write each word.

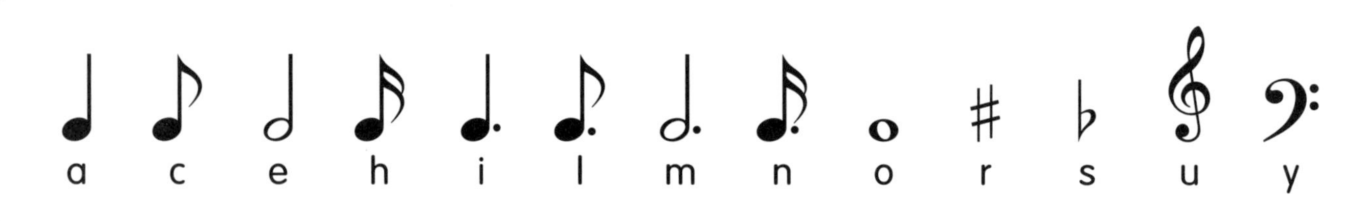

1. _____ _____ _____ _____ _____ _____ _____

2. _____ _____ _____ _____ _____

3. _____ _____ _____ _____ _____ _____ _____ _____ _____ _____

4. _____ _____ _____ _____ _____ _____ _____

5. _____ _____ _____ _____ _____ _____

   Spelling Games and Activities • EMC 8273 • © Evan-Moor Corporation

Musical Riddles

Name ________________________

Write the spelling word to solve the rhyming riddle.

> bugle   conductor   melody   recital   lullaby

1. On a stage or on a train, I'm still leading just the same.

   ____

2. Of all the sounds in a song, this is the part where you sing along.

   ____

3. You've practiced quite a lot; show the audience what you've got.

   ____

4. This instrument, with its sound so pure, will wake you up, that's for sure!

   ____

5. At the end of the day if my eyes won't close, this song will relax me from my head to my toes.

   ____

Name ________________________

Musical Clues

Read the clue. Write a spelling word to solve it.

> choir   chord   lullaby   rehearsal   songwriter

1. I'm a compound word.

   ____

2. I contain a sense.

   ____

3. I rhyme with **wire**.

   ____

4. I sound the same as the part that connects a lamp to the wall.

   ____

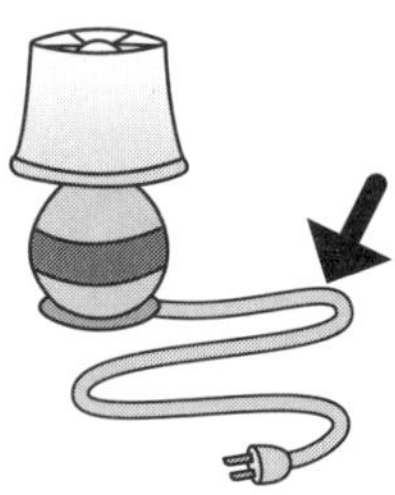

5. I have a **long i** sound, but you won't see an **i** in my name.

   ____

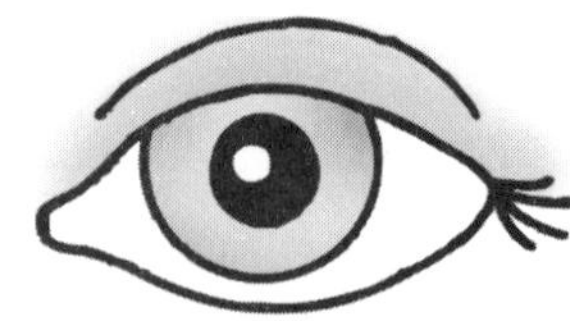

Spelling Games and Activities • EMC 8273 • © Evan-Moor Corporation

Name _______________________

Edit My Song

Misspelling a word is like singing a wrong note in a song. Read the song.
Five of the words are misspelled. Circle them and write them correctly
on the lines below.

_________________   _________________   _________________

_________________   _________________

Sing a Word

Name ___________________

Students work in pairs to write new lyrics to a familiar song using spelling words.

What You Need

- Words and Songs on page 79
- Song Sheet on page 80
- pencils

What You Do

1. Put students in pairs. Distribute 2 Words and Songs and a Song Sheet to each pair.

2. Explain to students that they will write new words to an old tune. The song's new words should include a spelling word and also spell the word out in the song. Sing the example for them:

   Example I'll change the words of "Mary Had a Little Lamb" and include the word **talent**:

   Gabriel has a talent, a talent, a talent.

   He plays the piano, t-a-l-e-n-t.

3. Choose a simple tune that the class knows (see the list of folk songs on page 79) or have students choose one. Each pair can write words to the same song, or they can each choose their own. Show them how to use the Song Sheet to plan and write their song.

4. Have students practice singing or saying their new song together in rhythm. When they are ready, have them perform their spelling song for the class.

   Bonus Get together in a larger group and change a longer song to include as many spelling words as you can!

Name ___________________________

Words and Songs

Use these words in your songs:

melody	chorus	songwriter
harmony	choir	recital
symphony	composer	rehearsal
lullaby	conductor	musical
chord	performer	bugle

Suggested Folk Songs

♪ Row, Row, Row Your Boat

♪ Skip to My Lou

♪ Take Me Out to the Ballgame

♪ She'll Be Coming 'Round the Mountain

♪ Mary Had a Little Lamb

♪ On Top of Old Smoky

♪ Home on the Range

♪ The Water Is Wide

♪ Kookaburra

♪ You Are My Sunshine

Song Sheet

Name ______________________________

Name ______________________________

Song to rewrite: ______________________________

Spelling word to use: ______________________________

Idea space

Our spelling song:

____

____

____

____

READ ALL ABOUT IT!

Practice spelling and using publishing words that name parts of a newspaper and the people who make it.

- ☐ article
- ☐ column
- ☐ comics
- ☐ caption
- ☐ interview
- ☐ opinion
- ☐ headline
- ☐ deadline
- ☐ accuracy
- ☐ source
- ☐ reporter
- ☐ editor
- ☐ publisher
- ☐ typesetter
- ☐ proofreader

SPELLING TIPS

⭐ A vowel before an **r** changes its sound from short or long to **r-controlled**. Example: **paper**

⭐ The letter **c** usually has a **soft** sound before **e**, **i**, or **y**: **typeface**. It usually has a **hard** sound before other letters: **fact**.

⭐ Vowel teams, such as **ew** and **ea**, have sounds of their own. They can be different from any of the letters in the team. Examples: n**ew**s, r**ea**d

⭐ Most words with more than one syllable have a **schwa** sound. There is no rule for which vowel to use to spell it.

Name _______________________

From Idea to Print

Make a path for the story idea to appear in a newspaper. Color the squares that have an **r**-controlled vowel sound.

START	column	accuracy	proofreader	reporter
reporter	deadline	editor	comics	editor
source	interview	typesetter	caption	publisher
deadline	comics	headline	article	accuracy
caption	editor	source	proofreader	opinion
opinion	typesetter	column	deadline	headline
opinion	interview	publisher	article	END

Name ______________________

Investigate the Words

The words in each group have something in common, but one of them looks or sounds different. Say each spelling word out loud. Then look at the letters in each word. Find the difference and answer the questions.

1. comics   article   source

How do these words **look** alike? ________________________________

Which one **sounds** different? ________________________________

How is it different? ________________________________

2. reporter   editor   publisher

How do these words **sound** alike? ________________________________

Which one **looks** different? ________________________________

How is it different? ________________________________

3. proofreader   opinion   headline

How are these words alike? ________________________________

Which one is different? ________________________________

How is it different? ________________________________

Name _______________________

News Clues

Write a spelling word to solve each riddle.

accuracy	article	caption	column
comics	deadline	editor	headline
proofreader	publisher	source	typesetter

1. **NEWS**

I have a silent consonant. Who am I?

____

2. **NEWS**

I have both a **hard c** and a **soft c**. Who am I?

____

3. **NEWS**

I have two different letters that sound the same. Who am I?

____

4. **NEWS**

I have a **long i** sound but no **i** in my name. Who am I?

____

More Than News

Look at this page from a newspaper.
Label each part.

caption   comics   headline
interview   opinion   reporter

County Fair Starts Today!

written by Ali Chatterjee

The County Fair begins today at Canyon Fairgrounds and runs through Sunday. The fair has something for everyone. There are rides and games, a parade with marching bands, and a pie-eating contest! Come see crafts and farm-grown fruits, vegetables, and animals. See who won a ribbon!

Nate Vega and his sheep at the county fair

Meet the Mayor

I talked with the new Grassville mayor, Latisha Coe, about her plans for our town.

Me: You've lived here for 10 years. What is our biggest challenge?

Mayor Coe: We've been growing, but we have more traffic and pollution now.
(continued on p. 8)

What Do You Think?

Our Town Council has talked about buying outdoor lights for the school so they can play sports after dark. I think it's great for kids to compete, but these games will be noisy for people who live nearby. Also, the lights will bother the farm animals and wildlife that want to sleep when the sun goes down. I don't want my chickens to be too tired to lay!

A Dog's Life

Name ___________________

Big Assignment

Katie is a newspaper reporter. Read her assignment. Some of the words are missing letters. Write the missing letters. Cross off each letter after you use it.

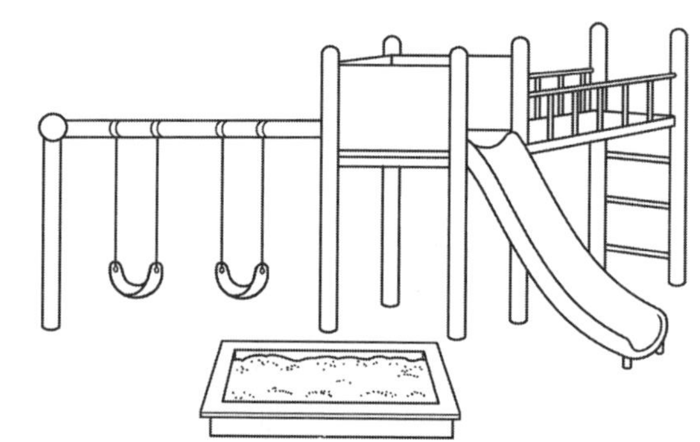

a	a	c	c	c	c	e	e
e	e	e	i	l	o	r	

New message — ⤢ ✕

To **Katie**

Subject **Assignment**

I need you to write an arti______ ______ ______ on the new playground. The planner

of the playground is a good sour______ ______ for information. Interv______ ______w

her for your story. Write a good h______ ______dline to get readers' attention.

Take photos of the playground and write a ______aption for each one.

Your d______ ______dline is Friday morning. Your story should fill three ______olumns.

Anupam, Edit______ ______-in-chief

Send A 〡 🔗 ☺ 🖼 ⋮ 🗑

 Spelling Games and Activities • EMC 8273 • © Evan-Moor Corporation

Name _______________________

News You Can Use

The reporters at the Baxter Bulletin Board are discussing story ideas.
Read each idea. Circle any misspelled words. Write them below.

comics ____

____

____

Name _______________________

Be a Typesetter

Students find the letter tiles needed to spell words and then proofread each other's work.

What You Need

- Read All About It! spelling word list on page 81
- Typesetting Tiles on page 89
- Word Trays on page 90

How to Play

The object of the game is to spell words using typesetting tiles.

1. Print one copy of the typesetting tiles for each student and cut them apart. Print enough copies of the word tray sheet for each student to have one tray. Distribute one set of typesetting tiles and one word tray to each student.

2. Explain to students that before there were typesetting machines, typesetters prepared the text by hand for printed books and newspapers. They picked up a metal piece for each letter and put them in order to make each word. Students will use their tiles to make words this way.

3. The teacher is the Word Caller for the first round. The Word Caller chooses a word from the spelling word list and tells the players the word.

4. Players spell the word with their typesetting tiles on their word tray as quickly as they can. When finished, they raise a hand and say, "Proofread!"

5. The Word Caller proofreads the spelling of one player with a raised hand.

   - If the word is spelled correctly, that player becomes the next Word Caller.

   - If the word is not spelled correctly, the Word Caller chooses another player and checks his or her spelling.

6. Continue until all words have been typeset or until all students have had a chance to be the Word Caller.

Typesetting Tiles

A	A	A	A	A	A	A	B	B	C
C	C	C	C	C	C	C	D	D	D
D	D	D	E	E	E	E	E	E	E
E	E	E	E	E	E	E	E	E	E
F	F	H	H	I	I	I	I	I	I
I	I	I	I	I	L	L	L	L	L
M	M	N	N	N	N	N	N	N	O
O	O	O	O	O	O	O	O	O	P
P	P	P	P	P	R	R	R	R	R
R	R	R	R	R	R	R	R	S	S
S	S	T	T	T	T	T	T	T	T
U	U	U	U	V	V	W	W	Y	Y

Word Trays

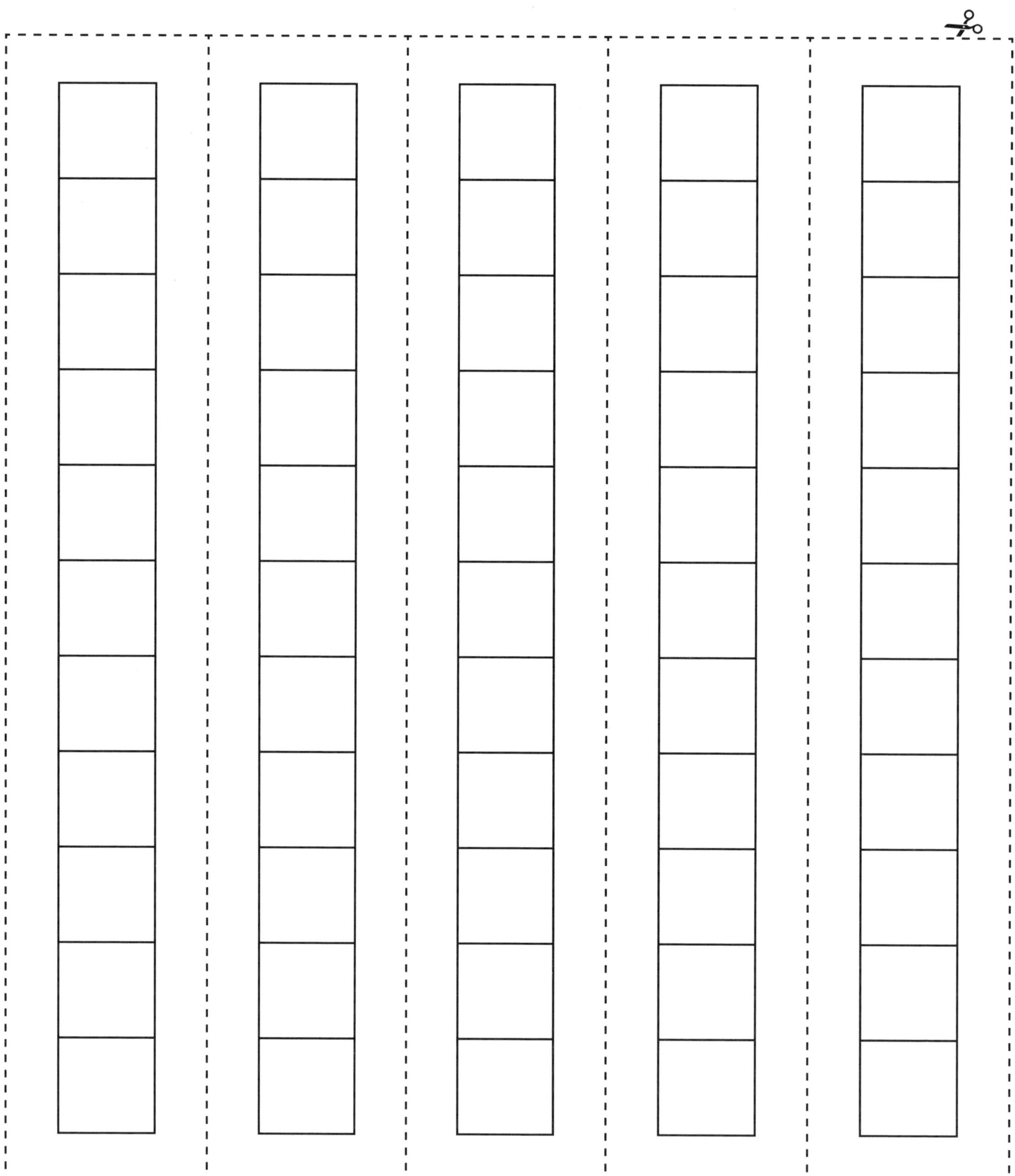

Spelling Games and Activities • EMC 8273 • © Evan-Moor Corporation

Extra Practice Worksheets

This section provides an additional 441 words to give students even more practice with spelling patterns and word study! The activity pages in this section can be used independently or to enhance *Building Spelling Skills* weekly lessons.

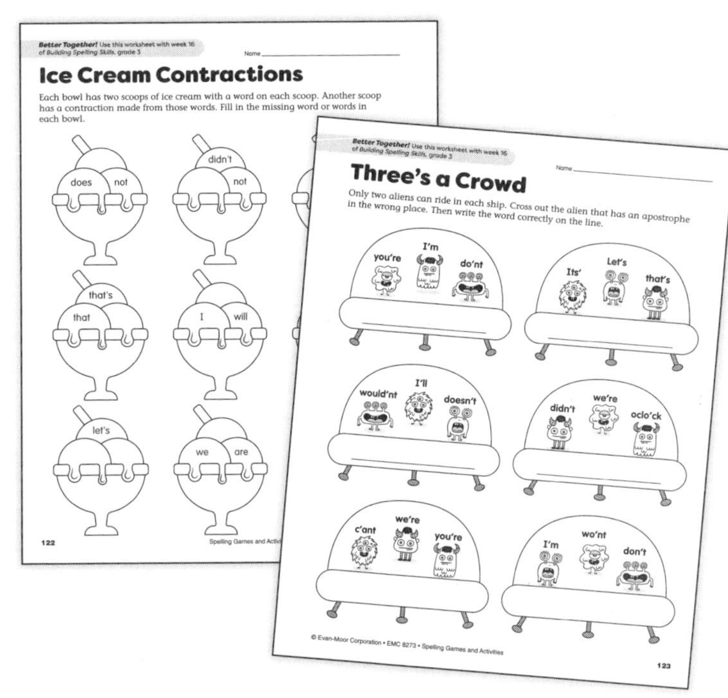

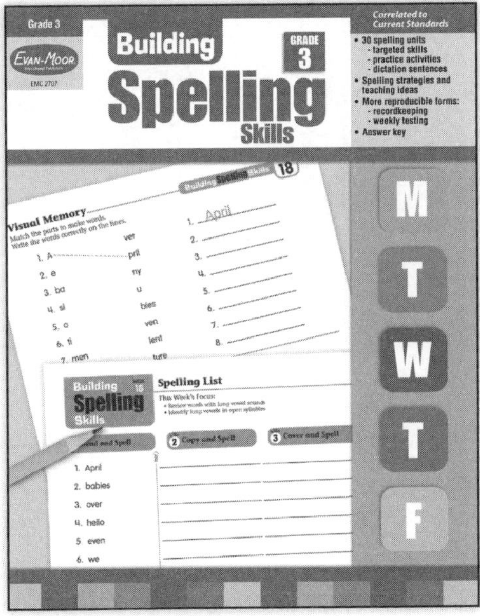

Better Together!

The worksheets in this section correspond to each week in *Building Spelling Skills*, grade 3.

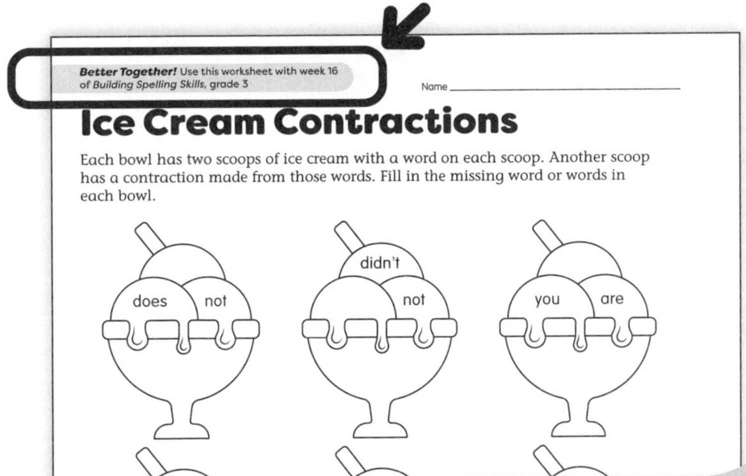

Name _______________________

Spelling Competition

Read each word. Decide what kind of **a** sound the word has. Use the chart to find out how many points each **a** sound gets. Some words have more than one **a** sound! Write each word's score.

Sound	Points
short **a**	1
long **a** spelled with an **a**	2
long **a** spelled with an **e**	3
schwa **ə**	4
other sound spelled with an **a**	5

1. afraid

Score

____

2. always

Score

____

3. catch

Score

____

4. eight

Score

____

5. playing

Score

____

6. prey

Score

____

7. than

Score

____

8. takes

Score

____

9. they

Score

____

Spelling Games and Activities • EMC 8273 • © Evan-Moor Corporation

Name ___________________________

Rhyme Time

Write a word from the box to finish the rhyme.

> ask   away   great   said   stand   waved

1. "I'm home!" Jamal _______________.

   "I'm going to bed."

2. "What is that?" I _______________.

   Joy replies, "It's a mask."

3. This funny library book was _______________.

   Let's take it back now so I won't be late!

4. Ali's best friend is moving _______________.

   They can't play together after today.

5. Look at the musicians in the band.

   The horn players sit, but the

   drummers _______________.

6. There goes my neighbor, who smiled

   and _______________.

   She's walking her dog, who is so well behaved.

Name ___________________________

Scrambled Words

Unscramble the letters on each scrambled egg to spell
a word from the box.

been	help	left	many	next	very

1.

____

2.

____

3.
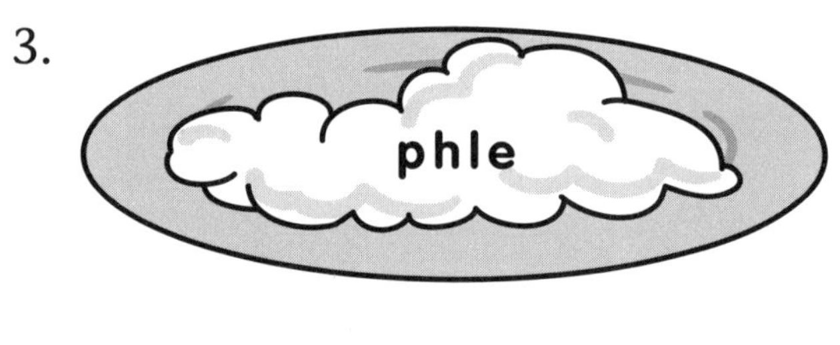

____

4.

____

5.

____

6.

____

Trees and Leaves

Each word in the box has a **long e** sound. If the **long e** is spelled with **ee**,
write the word on the tree trunk. If it is spelled with **ea**, write the word on a leaf.
If it is spelled another way, write it at the tree's roots.

| believe | between | easy | leave | please | sea | seen | she | three |

Name _______________________

Secret Code

Use the code of shapes to write each word.

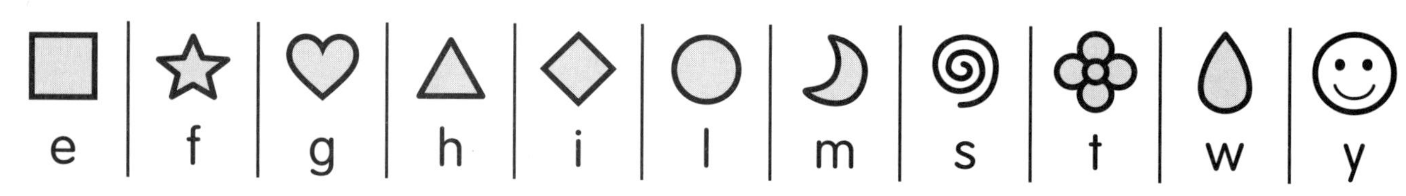

1. ○ ◇ ☆ □

   ____ ____ ____ ____

2. ＠ ◊ ◇ ☽

   ____ ____ ____ ____

3. ◊ △ ◇ ○ □

   ____ ____ ____ ____ ____

4. ◊ △ ☺

   ____ ____ ____

5. ○ ◇ ♡ △ ✿

   ____ ____ ____ ____ ____

6. □ ☺ □

   ____ ____ ____

Name _______________________________

Dog Poem

Read the poem. Write rhyming words from the box to finish the poem.

buy	drink	eye	find	I	kind
my	pitch	swim	try	which	why

A man looked low and high

for a dog that he could _________________.

When asked what _________________

of dog did he _________________,

"It's a dog with a patch on one _________________."

Name _______________________

Missing Letters

The vowels in these words ran away! Finish each word using these letters or
letter pairs: **a, e, ew, o, oa, ow**.

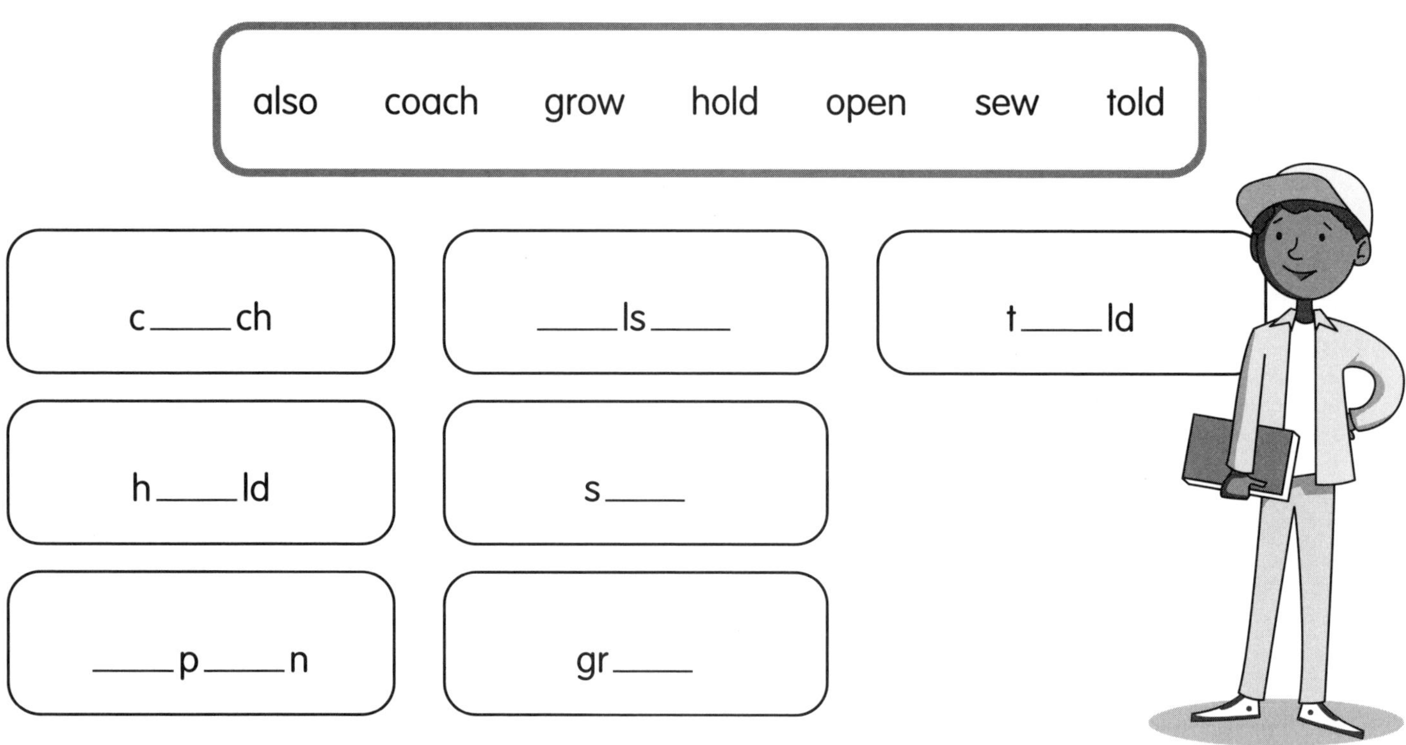

also   coach   grow   hold   open   sew   told

c____ch

____ls____

t____ld

h____ld

s____

____p____n

gr____

Some of the consonants in these words ran away! Finish each word using these
letters or letter pairs: **ck, st, t, th**.

almost   both   most   often   pocket   rocket   throne

mo____

bo____

of____en

____rone

ro____et

almo____

po____et

Name ______________________

Crossroads

Write each of these words in pairs that share a letter.
Cross out each word as you use it.

almost	also	~~both~~	coach
grow	hold	~~most~~	often
open	pocket	rocket	sew
throne	told		

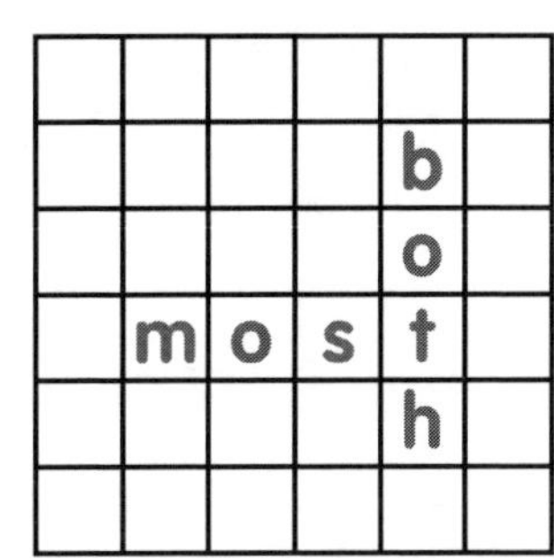

1.

2.

3.

4.

5.

6.

99

Name ______________________________

Alike and Different

The words in each group have something in common, but one of them looks or
sounds different. Say each spelling word out loud. Then look at the letters in each
word. Find the difference and answer the questions.

(**Example**)   cute   fuel   use

How do these words **sound** alike? _______ All have a long u sound. _______

Which one **looks** different? _____________ fuel _____________

How is it different? _______ It doesn't end in a silent e. _______

---

1. **under   unit   use**

How do these words **look** alike? _____________________________________

Which one **sounds** different? _____________________________________

How is it different? _____________________________________

---

2. **few   new   you**

How do these words **sound** alike? _____________________________________

Which one **looks** different? _____________________________________

How is it different? _____________________________________

---

3. **much   such   touch**

How do these words **sound** alike? _____________________________________

Which one **looks** different? _____________________________________

How is it different? _____________________________________

          Spelling Games and Activities • EMC 8273 • © Evan-Moor Corporation

Name ___________________________

Follow the Clue Path

Read the first clue. Draw a line to the ● near the best answer.
Then read the next clue. See what shape the lines make.

START

Clue: Find a word that sounds like "you're."

●

●

Answer
young

New clue: Find a word for a "grown-up boy" inside another word.

●

Answer
music

New clue: Find a word that is the opposite of "old."

●

Answer
your

New clue: Find a word that sounds like it is not feeling well.

●

Answer
human

New clue: Draw a line to START. If all your answers are correct, your shape is part of that word!

Name ___________________________

Cake for U!

Oh, look at all the cakes! Each one has a different way to spell the **long u** sound. Each person is holding the first letter or letters of a word that ends with a **long u** sound. Draw a line to match each person with his or her cake.

blew   blue   do   to   too   two

_____ew

_____o

_____oo

t

bl

_____o

d

_____o

_____ue

t

bl

tw

Name ___________________

The Living Gift

Read the story. Eight of the words are misspelled.
Cross them out and write them correctly above the word.

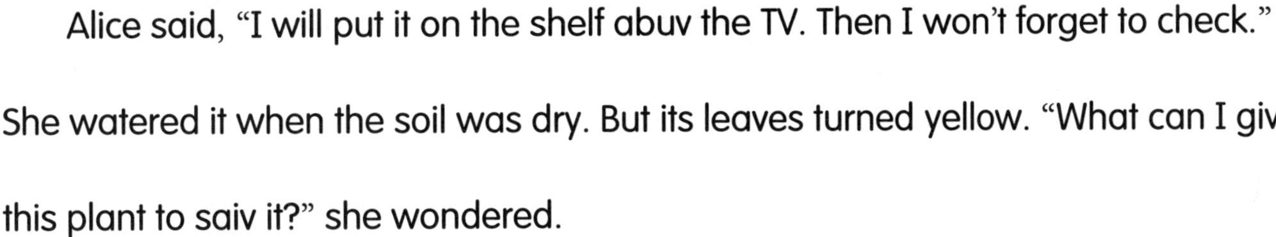

Alice looked sadly at the plant she got for her birthday.

It had flowers then. Uncle Tim said, "It needs water to stay alive.

You hav to water it when it is dry."

Alice said, "I will put it on the shelf abuv the TV. Then I won't forget to check."

She watered it when the soil was dry. But its leaves turned yellow. "What can I giv

this plant to saiv it?" she wondered.

One day, Alice's family had lunch at Uncle Tim's home. She said, "That's the

same kind of plant I have. They used to look ulike, but now they don't. I don't no

what is wrong with it." Uncle Tim said he would come over to look at it.

"Oh, I see the problem!" said Uncle Tim when he arrived. "The plant needs

more sunlight to liv. Moove it near a window." Alice put it on the kitchen table.

The leaves started to turn green again. A few weeks later,

another flower bloomed!

Name ______________________

Seeing Double

Draw a line to match the first and second halves of each word
to make a whole pair of binoculars. Write the word on the line.

Hint: Each word was split between its double consonants.

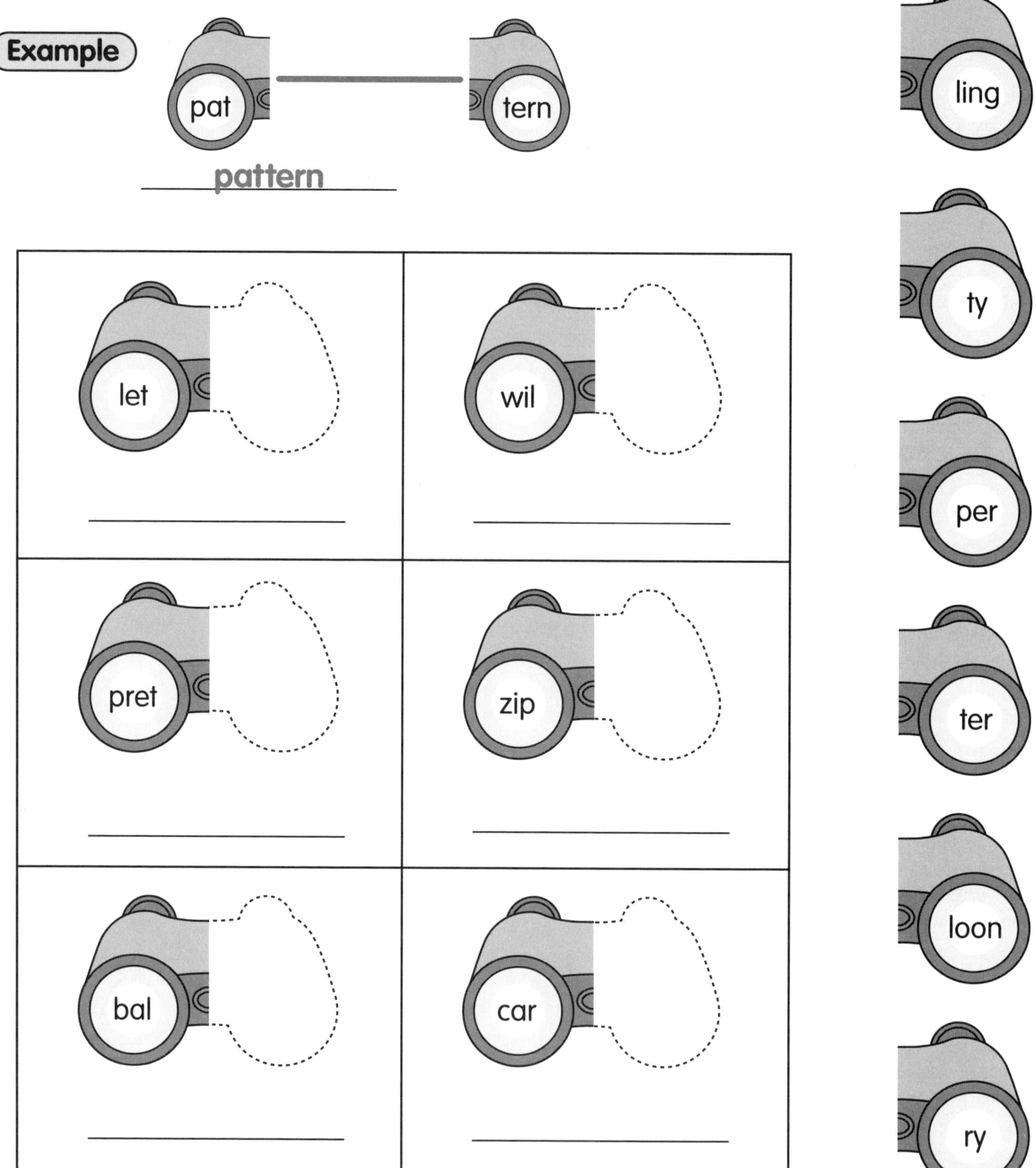

Hidden Words

Look at the letters in each spelling word. Use them to make other words. Write them in the tree. The first one is done for you.

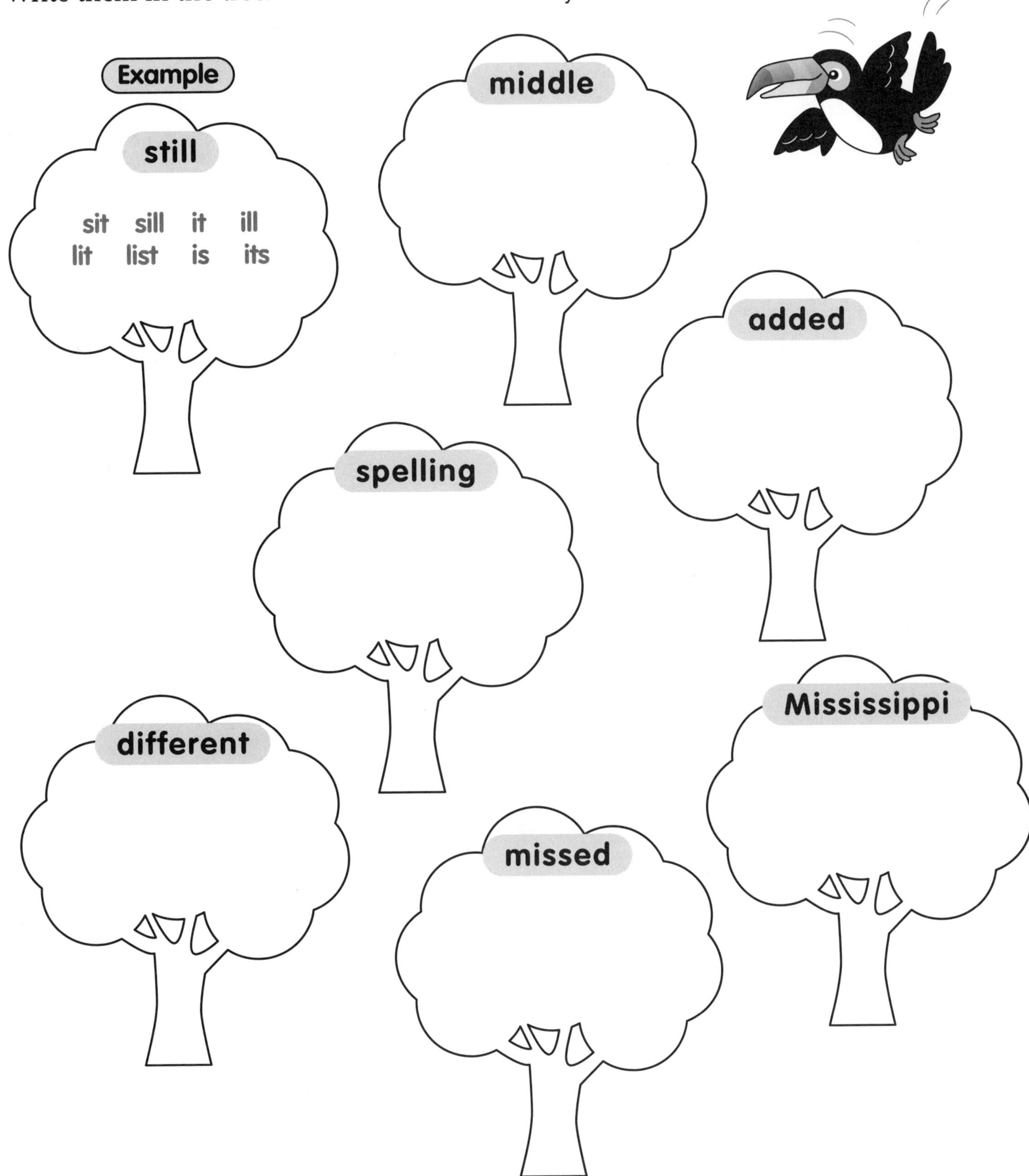

Name ___________________________

Spot the Misspelling

One word in each group below is spelled incorrectly. Find the word and spell it
correctly in the spaces below the group. Then write the numbered letters in the
matching spaces of the riddle to answer it.

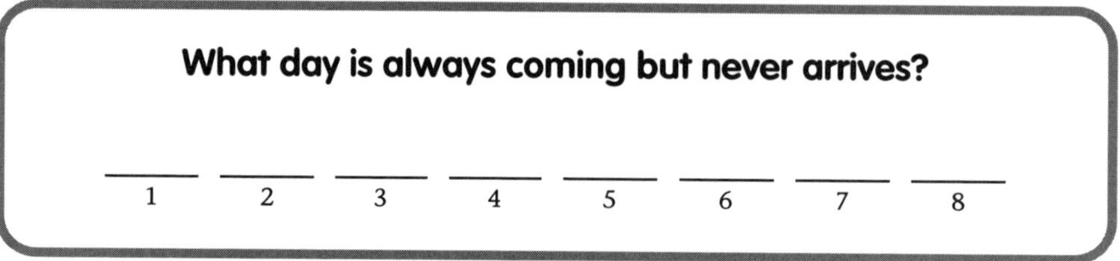

1. joked, ended, smileed

   ___ ___ ___ ___ ___ ___
        3

2. comming, doing, having

   ___ ___ ___ ___ ___ ___
        7

3. geting, started, smiling

   ___ ___ ___ ___ ___ ___ ___
                  1

4. swimming, recieved, happening

   ___ ___ ___ ___ ___ ___ ___ ___
    5

5. swam, jokeed, doing

   ___ ___ ___ ___ ___
        4

6. ended, having, startted

   ___ ___ ___ ___ ___ ___ ___
                6

7. received, swiming, happened

   ___ ___ ___ ___ ___ ___ ___
        8

8. joked, swam, duing

   ___ ___ ___ ___ ___
        2

Name ___________________________

Action Word Riddles

Write the spelling word to solve the rhyming riddle.

came	doing	ended	happened	having
joked	received	smiled	started	swam

1. You got from here to there but not through the air.

   ___________________ (has one syllable)

2. You turned your frown upside down.

   ___________________ (has a silent **e**)

3. Dad was kidding when he told us to spend all day knitting.

   ___________________ (ends in a **t** sound)

4. You asked for some clay and got it today.

   ___________________ (has a vowel digraph)

5. When it's fall and cool, you've gone back to school.

   ___________________ (ends in an **əd** sound)

6. When the day was done, you said "bye" to the sun.

   ___________________ (uses only 3 letters)

7. I called on the phone; now you're at my home.

   ___________________ (has a **hard c** sound)

8. Your body's in bed with a dream in your head.

   ___________________ (has a **v**)

9. When you saw his sad face, you asked what took place.

   ___________________ (has a double letter)

10. Working or playing on the lawn, it's fun with a lot going on.

   ___________________ (has a **long u** sound)

Name _______________________________

What Word Am I?

Write a spelling word to solve each riddle.

close	cube	mean	might	niece
price	these	tried	uniform	usually

1. I have a **soft c**, and I'm part of a family.

   ____

2. I look like I start with a pronoun, but I don't sound like I do.

   ____

3. I have a **long u**, and you wear me.

   ____

4. I have 3 consonants, but none of them sounds like its name.

   ____

5. I start with a **hard c**, and I end with a short verb.

   ____

6. I have a **long i** sound made by only one vowel.

   ____

Buddy Words

Read each word. Find a buddy word from the word box.
Then think of another buddy word and write it.

A buddy word rhymes, and its vowel sound is spelled the same way.

Example day, way, tray

brain	close	float	mean	might
price	show	stayed	tried	

From the box   **Your word**

1. played _______________________ _______________________

2. rain _______________________ _______________________

3. boat _______________________ _______________________

4. grow _______________________ _______________________

5. cried _______________________ _______________________

6. right _______________________ _______________________

7. nice _______________________ _______________________

8. nose _______________________ _______________________

9. clean _______________________ _______________________

Name ___________________

Use Your Clues

Look closely at the starting, ending, and vowel sounds of the clue words in the example. They describe a secret word in the box. The secret word will have the same sounds, but the spelling may be different from the clue words.

| children | finish | push | short | sure |
| think | where | who | whole | with |

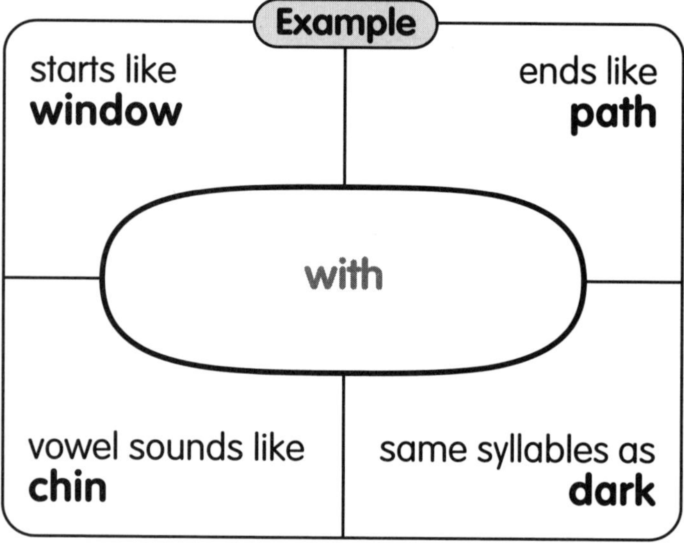

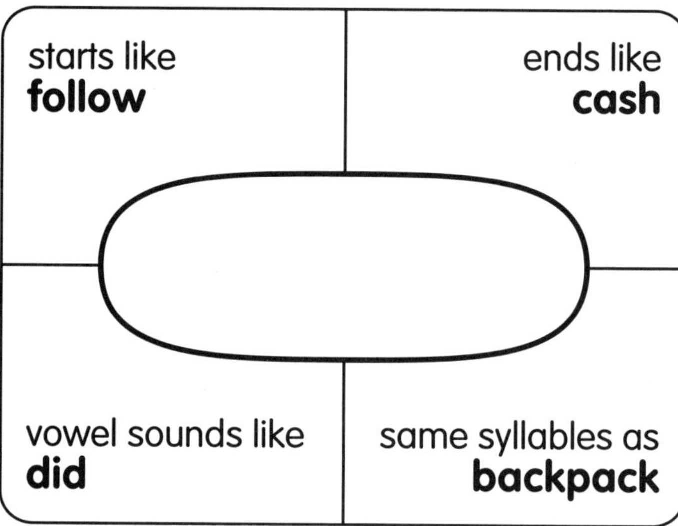

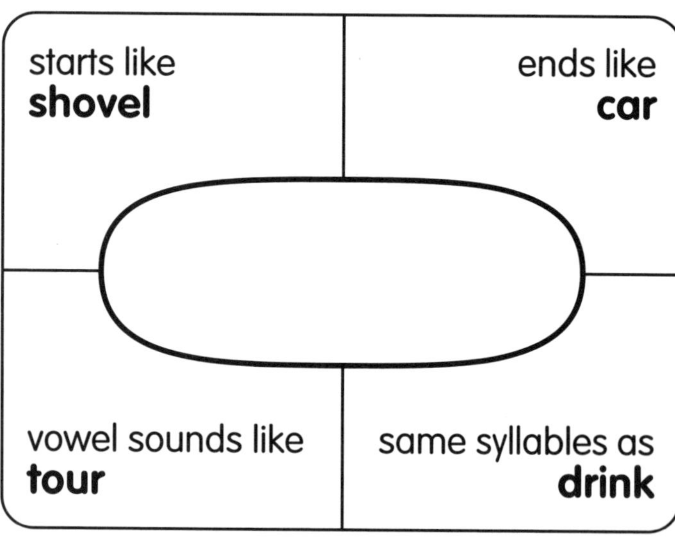

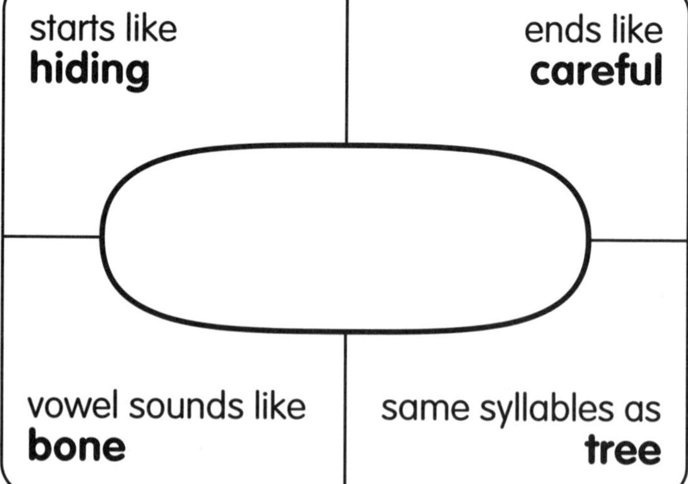

Name ______________________________

Changing Words

Read the silly phrase. Unscramble each phrase to write a spelling word
on the line.

> everywhere   reached   search
>
> teacher   together   where

1. we her   ______________________

2. ad cheer   ______________________

3. greet hot   ______________________

4. she car   ______________________

5. were he very   ______________________

6. the race   ______________________

Name ______________________

Spelling Puzzle

Cut apart the puzzle pieces. Use them to complete page 113.

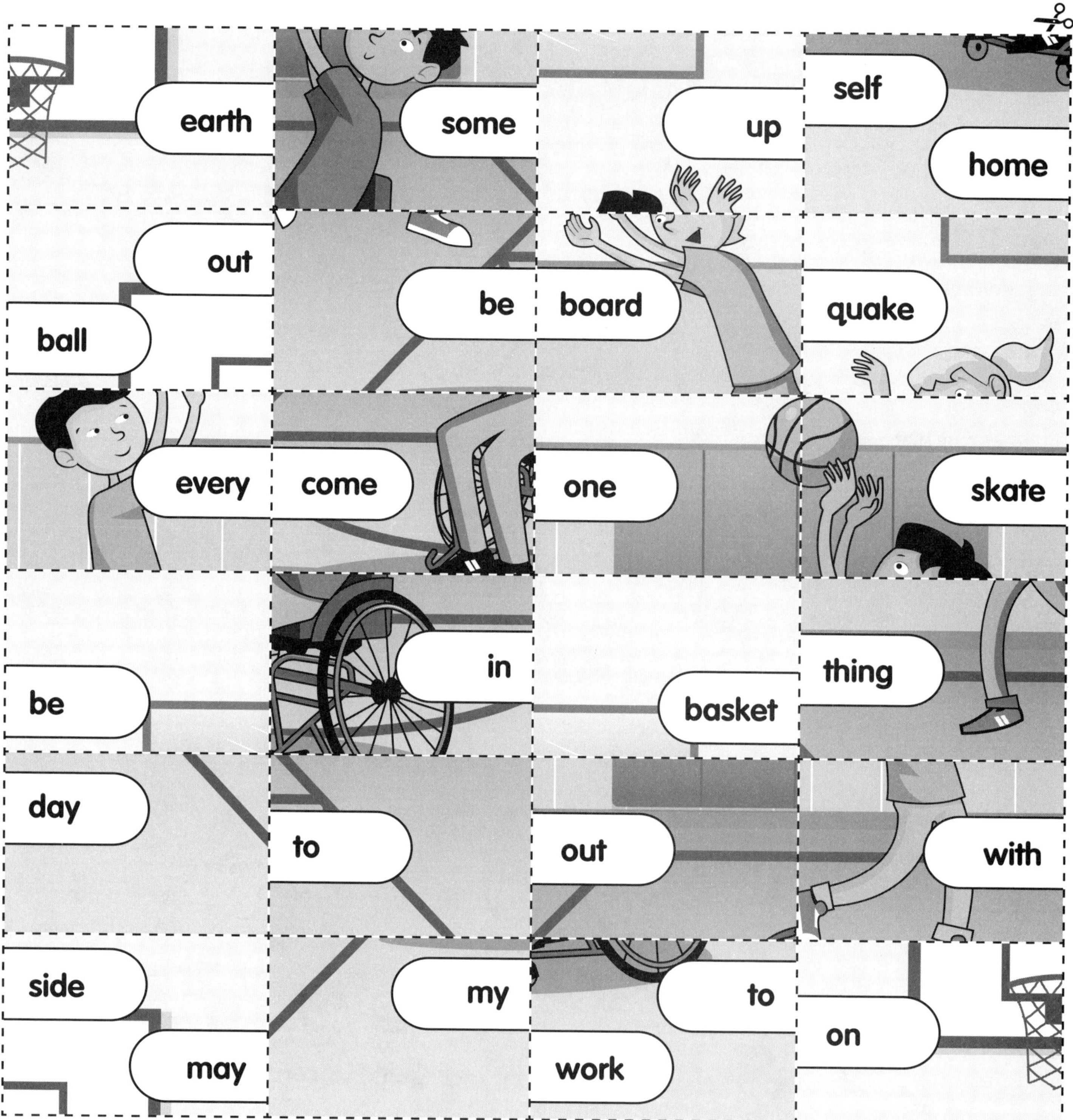

Spelling Games and Activities • EMC 8273 • © Evan-Moor Corporation

Name _______________________

Spelling Puzzle, *continued*

Put the puzzle pieces together to make words. Then move them
to make a picture of a sport. Glue them together below.

glue	glue	glue	glue
glue	glue	glue	glue
glue	glue	glue	glue
glue	glue	glue	glue
glue	glue	glue	glue
glue	glue	glue	glue

Name ___________________________

Play Ball!

The players have shown up for practice. The vowel sound in each player's nickname is spelled the same as his or her sport. Draw a line from each player to the correct practice field.

Mall

Straw

Small

Strongest

Soccer

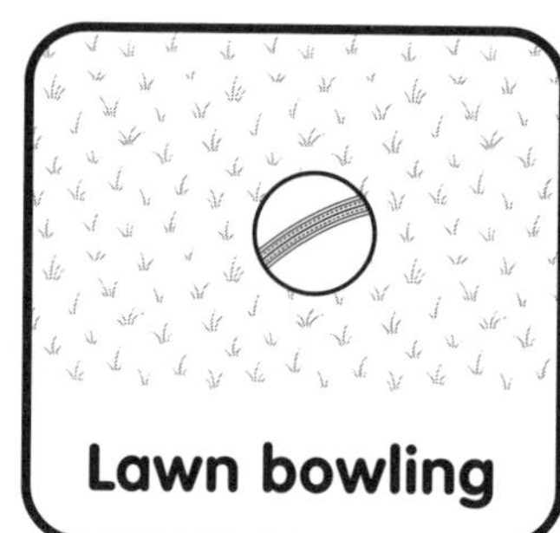

Lawn bowling

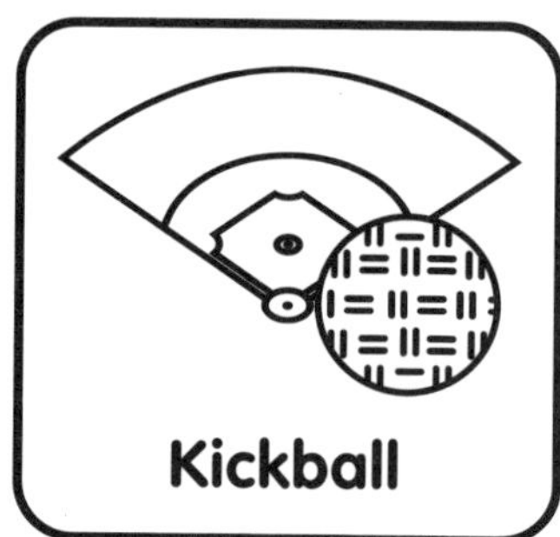

Kickball

Longer

Along

Falling

Drawing

Alike and Different

The words in each group have something in common, but one of them looks or sounds different. Say each spelling word out loud. Then look at the letters in each word. Find the difference and answer the questions.

(**Example**)   **bought   called   brought**

How do these words **sound** alike? __________ All have a short o sound. __________

Which one **looks** different? __________ called __________

How is it different? __________ Its vowel sound is spelled with an a. __________

---

1. **bought   rough   tough**

How do these words **look** alike? ________________________________

Which one **sounds** different? ________________________________

How is it different? ________________________________

---

2. **called   song   bought**

How do these words **sound** alike? ________________________________

Which one **looks** different? ________________________________

How is it different? ________________________________

---

3. **brought   tough   bought**

How do these words **look** alike? ________________________________

Which one **sounds** different? ________________________________

How is it different? ________________________________

Name ___________________________

Letter Delivery

Lee the Letter Carrier drives to every home in her neighborhood. She drops off letters to each home and picks up letters to mail out. Help her drop letters off the ends of some words and pick up a different ending.

Example

Drop off letter: ________ y ________

Add **ies**: ________ puppies ________

Drop off letter: ________________

Add **ies**: ________________

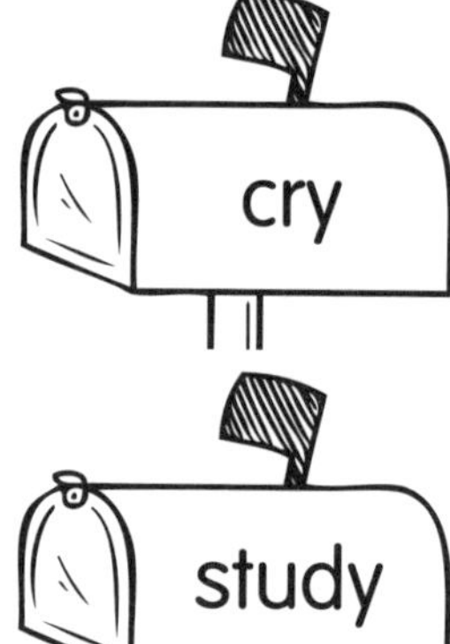

Drop off letter: ________________

Add **ied**: ________________

Add **ied**: ________________

Drop off letter: ________________

Add **s**: ________________

Add **s**: ________________

Name ____________________

Spelling Competition

Read each word. Decide what kind of **y** sound the
word has. Use the chart to find out how many points
each **y** sound gets. Write each word's score.

Sound	Points
long **e**	2
long **i**	4
in a diphthong	6
as a consonant	8

1. cry

Score

______

2. study

Score

______

3. story

Score

______

4. only

Score

______

5. toys

Score

______

6. finally

Score

______

7. family

Score

______

8. lady

Score

______

9. shy

Score

______

Name _________________________

Missing Letters

The vowels in these words ran away! Finish each word using these letters:
ew, **oo**, **u**, **ue**.

brook	chew	due	food	full	good	put	room	true

f____d

tr____

p____t

r____m

ch____

f____ll

d____

g____d

br____k

Some of the consonants in these words ran away! Finish each word using these
letters: **c**, **ch**, **d**, **k**, **t**, **th**.

cookie	football	looked	school	stood	truth

foo____ball

____oo____ie

tru____

stoo____

loo____e____

s____ool

Name ___________________________

Crossroads

Write each of these words in pairs that share a letter.
Cross out each word as you use it.

brook   chew   cookie   due

~~food~~   full   ~~good~~   looked

room   school   stood   put

true   truth

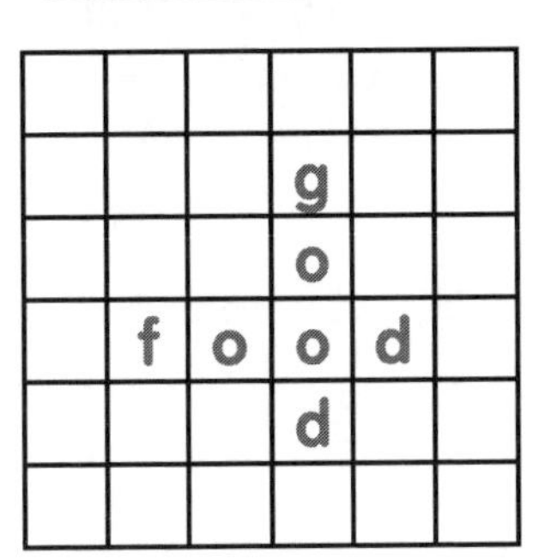

1.
2.
3.

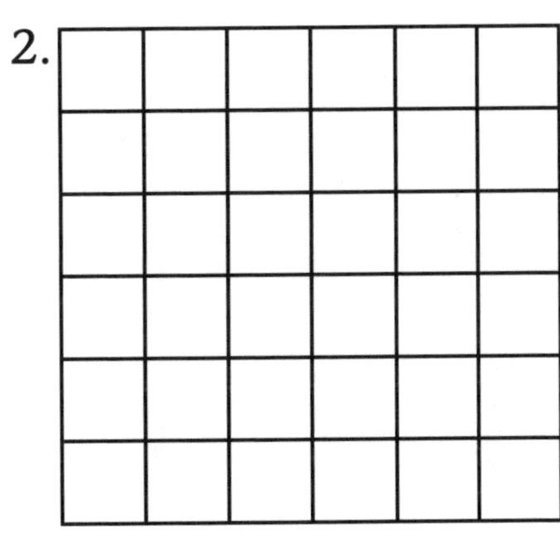
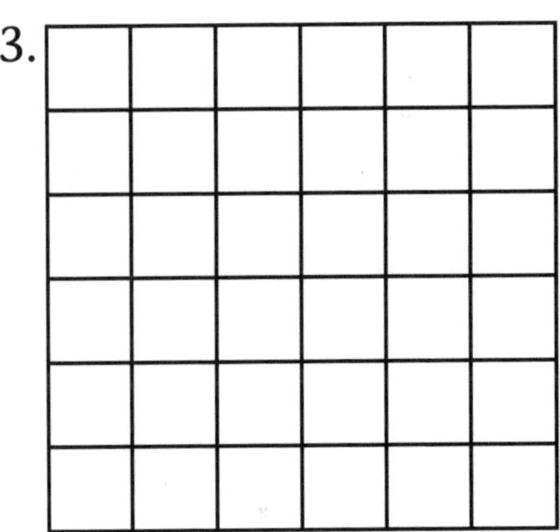

4.
5.
6.

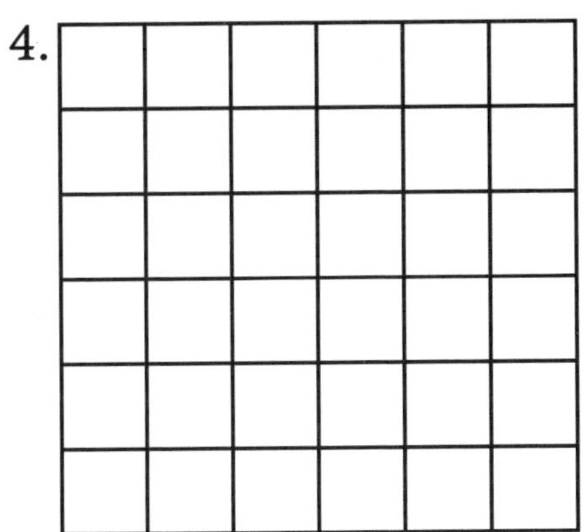
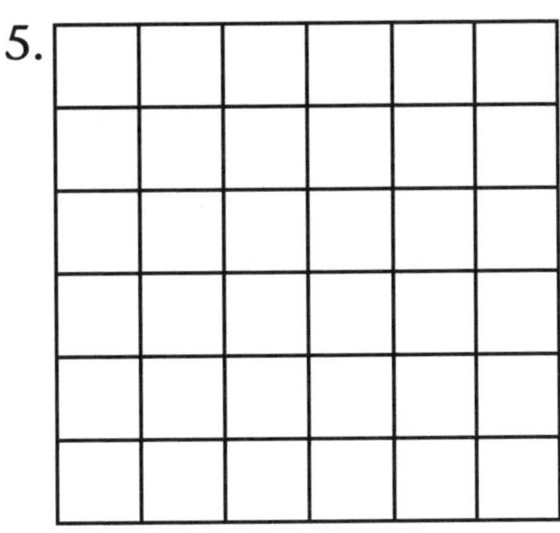
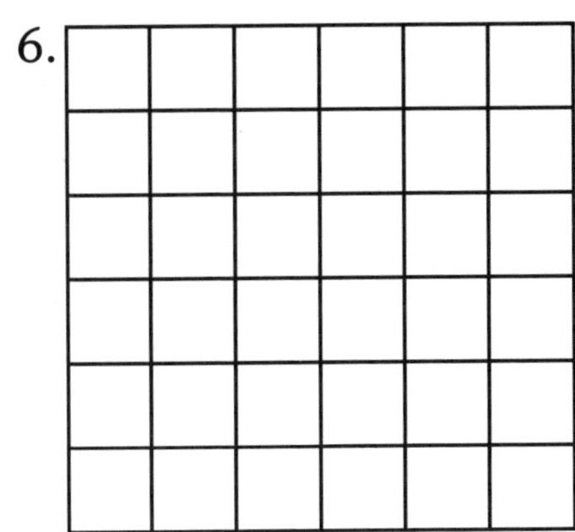

Name _______________________

Unscramble and Write

Unscramble these words that all have a syllable that rhymes with **toy**.

boy	choice	enjoy	joined	loyal
oily	pointing	poison	voyage	

yob   _______________________   allyo   _______________________

nitpingo   _______________________   spooni   _______________________

hiccoe   _______________________   ojney   _______________________

lyio   _______________________   edjion   _______________________

goavey   _______________________

Now write a story using at least 5 of these words.

____

____

____

____

____

____

Name _______________________

Sailing Across the C

Circle 10 words in the word search that have a **hard** or **soft c** sound,
a **ch** digraph, or an **e** that may be silent or heard. Words may go
forward, backward, up, or down.

chocolate	choice	choose	coin	destroy
enjoy	joined	oyster	voice	voyage

E	H	C	H	O	C	L	E	T	I	C	G	R	U	L
E	N	J	O	Y	P	N	I	B	S	H	H	L	A	O
G	L	A	U	R	N	E	P	O	C	U	R	H	E	W
A	F	R	A	V	O	P	H	E	M	S	N	I	O	C
Y	C	I	G	H	T	H	H	F	O	E	I	O	I	S
O	P	P	V	P	A	N	C	D	E	N	Y	O	J	K
V	H	H	M	P	H	R	H	N	U	W	S	D	D	O
P	C	O	E	T	A	L	O	C	O	H	C	E	I	I
L	H	T	W	S	R	G	I	O	E	C	P	O	S	N
I	O	N	Y	O	C	L	C	T	A	R	O	A	T	E
H	I	N	J	O	Y	U	E	F	N	E	T	T	R	U
P	S	A	N	G	W	O	C	S	O	H	A	J	O	H
U	E	P	R	E	R	O	D	E	S	T	R	O	Y	T
F	N	H	H	S	U	A	Y	R	T	A	R	I	D	I
A	O	Y	V	O	I	S	E	N	N	F	A	N	N	U
N	Y	B	H	O	N	U	L	V	O	I	C	E	H	O
F	S	L	G	H	O	T	O	F	O	U	H	D	R	A
E	T	F	L	C	S	R	U	M	M	O	E	O	I	A
L	E	O	M	T	O	I	S	T	E	R	H	S	U	V
R	R	V	O	Y	I	D	G	E	Y	W	F	O	U	G

Name _______________________

Ice Cream Contractions

Each bowl has two scoops of ice cream with a word on each scoop. Another scoop has a contraction made from those words. Fill in the missing word or words in each bowl.

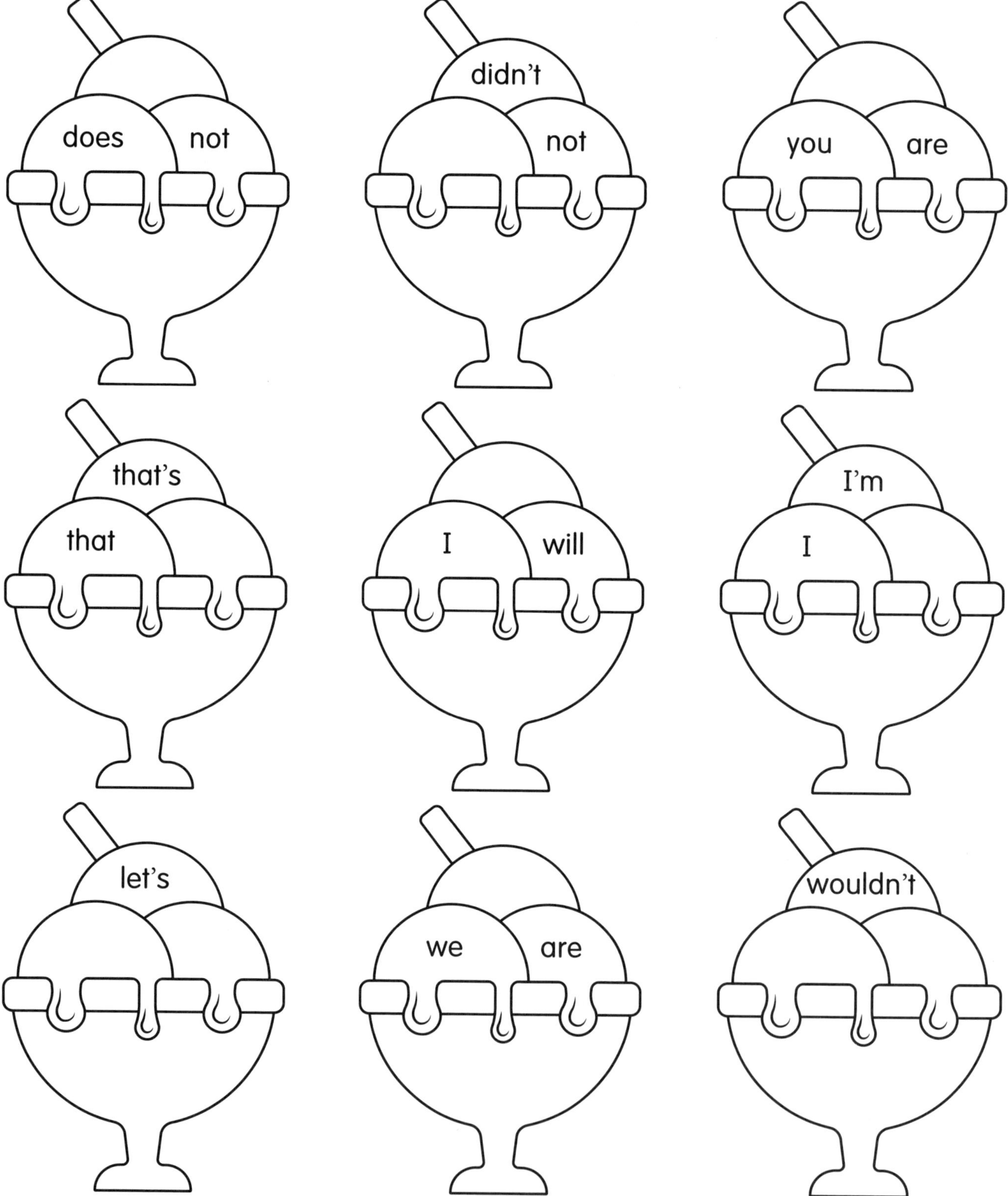

Spelling Games and Activities • EMC 8273 • © Evan-Moor Corporation

Three's a Crowd

Only two aliens can ride in each ship. Cross out the alien that has an apostrophe
in the wrong place. Then write the word correctly on the line.

Name _____________________

Spelling Competition

Read each word. Decide what different sounds the word has. Use the chart to find out how many points each sound gets. Write each word's score.

Sound	Points
vowel pair **ow**	1
vowel pair **ou**	2
begins with consonant blend	3
ends with consonant blend	4
schwa	5

1. ground   **Score** ______

2. grown   **Score** ______

3. about   **Score** ______

4. country   **Score** ______

5. around   **Score** ______

6. group   **Score** ______

7. own   **Score** ______

8. cousin   **Score** ______

9. follow   **Score** ______

Name ______________________

Scrambled Words

Unscramble the letters on each scrambled egg to spell a word from the box.

> below   found   house   should   town   would

1.

____

2.

____

3.

____

4.

____

5.

____

6.

____

Name _______________________

Word Race

Follow the directions to help the runners make a path to the end of their race.

Read each word out loud. Color the squares of words that have a **long a** or **long u** sound.

START

April	babies	silent	over	dear
hello	menu	tiny	even	white
tiny	future	raise	used	hello
those	dear	over	babies	those
white	even	we	future	raise

END

Read each word out loud. Color the squares of words that have a **long e**, **long i**, or **long o** sound.

START

silent	future	white	those	over
hello	April	tiny	raise	silent
over	even	we	used	white
raise	menu	future	April	even
babies	used	those	tiny	hello

END

Name ________________

Hidden Words

Look at the letters in each spelling word. Use them to make other words. Write them in the tree. The first one is done for you.

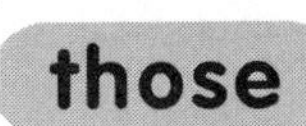

dear

those

April

babies

white

silent

Name _______________________

Rock, Paper, Scissors

Read the spelling word. Then look at the chart to see if the word is a rock, paper, or scissors. Circle the correct picture.

Word with a schwa or **short u** sound that is spelled with an **a**:  rock

Word with a schwa or **short u** sound that is spelled with an **e**:  paper

Word with a schwa or **short u** sound that is spelled with an **o**:  scissors

Then compare the two words in the same row. Write an **X** on the word that loses.

rock beats scissors   scissors beats paper   paper beats rock

1.
money

or

disagree

2.
again

or

problem

3.
of

or

silent

Name _______________________

Crossroads

Write each of these words in pairs that share a letter.
Cross out each word as you use it.

again	change	does	given
laid	lower	money	nice
other	read	some	tired

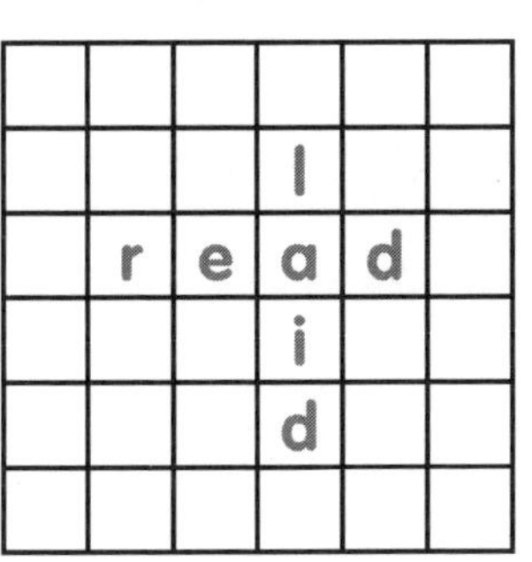

1.

2.

3.

4.

5.

6.

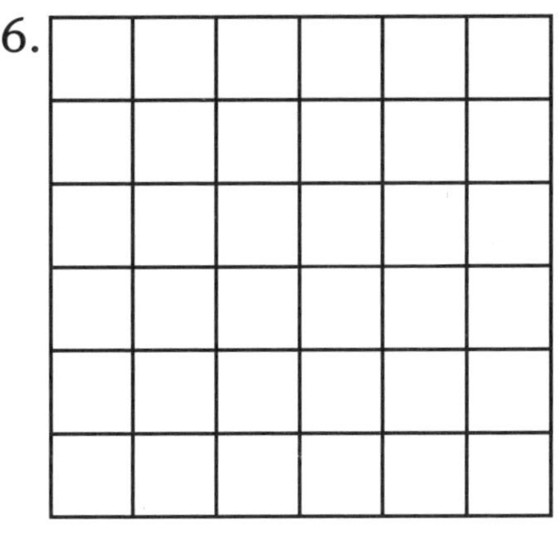

Name ___________________________

Which Animal?

Unscramble the letters to spell a word. Then say each word and listen to the sound of the **g**. Draw a line to the animal that has the same **g** sound.

| age | danger | giant | gone | goose | guard | guess | huge |

1. segus ___________________________

2. gheu ___________________________

3. ega ___________________________

4. taing ___________________________

5. oesog ___________________________

6. raudg ___________________________

7. oneg ___________________________

8. deagnr ___________________________

goat

hard g

giraffe

soft g

Name _______________________________

Which Animal?

Unscramble the letters to spell a word. Then say each word and listen to the sound of the **c**. Draw a line to the animal that has the same **c** sound.

carton	cereal	city	clean	coast	could	face

1. acef _______________________

2. saoct _______________________

3. tiyc _______________________

4. realec _______________________

5. duocl _______________________

6. lacen _______________________

7. tornca _______________________

cat

hard c

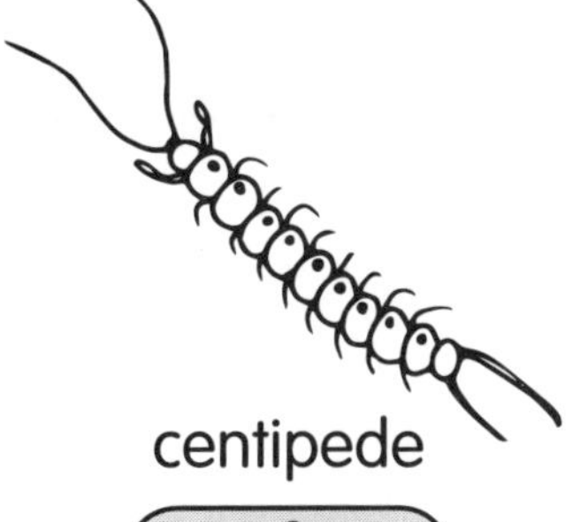

centipede

soft c

Name ___________________________

Missing Letters

Some of the vowels in these words ran away!
Write **o** or **u** to finish each word.

w_____rd

t_____rned

n_____rse

w_____rk

w_____rld

j_____ry

Some letters in these words ran away!
Write **ear**, **er**, or **ir** to finish each word.

w_____

h_____e

f_____e

st_____red

l_____n

b_____d

g_____l

w_____e

f_____st

   Spelling Games and Activities • EMC 8273 • © Evan-Moor Corporation

Name ___________________________

Rock, Paper, Scissors

Read the spelling word. Then look at the chart to see if the word is a rock, paper, or scissors. Circle the correct picture.

> Words with an **r**-controlled **i**: rock
>
> Words with an **r**-controlled **u**: paper
>
> Words with an **r**-controlled **o**: scissors

Then compare the two words in the same row. Write an **X** on the word that loses.

 beats     beats     beats

1.

bird      or   **word**   

2.

nurse or **first**

3.

jury      or   **world**   

Name ______________________________

Unscramble and Write

Unscramble these words that all have **r**-controlled vowels.

> aren't   before   care   farm   horse
>
> large   more   morning   partner   start

geral ________________________

rafm ________________________

hsore ________________________

rastt ________________________

febroe ________________________

roimngn ________________________

ermo ________________________

pentrar ________________________

crea ________________________

trane' ________________________

Now write a story using at least 5 of these words.

____

____

____

____

____

____

Spelling Games and Activities • EMC 8273 • © Evan-Moor Corporation

Name ___________________

Sailing Far

Circle 10 words in the word search that have an **r**-controlled vowel.
Words may go forward, backward, up, down, or diagonally.

before	chart	hard	horse	large
morning	north	partner	stare	warning

S	B	I	M	P	C	L	E	Y	I	E	G	R	A	L
I	E	J	O	Y	B	U	T	V	E	R	F	L	Y	O
H	F	W	U	R	N	E	P	G	N	I	N	R	O	W
G	A	A	A	V	O	P	H	O	R	S	W	E	R	C
A	R	R	G	R	T	H	H	F	O	E	S	O	I	L
L	P	N	D	P	A	N	C	D	E	N	T	O	J	A
V	H	I	M	P	H	H	H	N	U	W	A	D	D	S
P	C	N	E	T	A	A	O	C	O	H	R	E	I	E
L	H	G	N	I	N	R	O	M	E	C	E	O	S	N
K	I	W	E	O	C	T	C	H	R	E	O	A	T	E
H	A	N	T	O	Y	U	E	J	A	R	T	E	M	E
P	S	A	R	G	W	O	C	S	O	H	E	L	O	H
B	E	F	O	R	E	O	P	A	R	T	N	O	R	A
F	S	H	N	H	I	T	E	R	T	A	R	I	N	R
A	R	Y	V	O	I	S	E	C	H	A	R	T	I	E
N	O	B	L	O	N	U	L	V	T	I	C	E	N	D
F	H	L	A	H	O	T	O	F	R	U	H	D	R	A
E	T	F	R	C	S	R	U	M	O	O	E	O	I	A
L	E	O	J	T	P	A	R	T	N	E	R	S	U	V
Y	E	L	E	O	W	D	G	E	Y	W	F	O	U	G

Name ______________________________

Sweet Riddle

One word in each group below is spelled incorrectly. Find the word and spell it correctly in the spaces below the group. Then write the numbered letters in the matching spaces of the riddle to answer it.

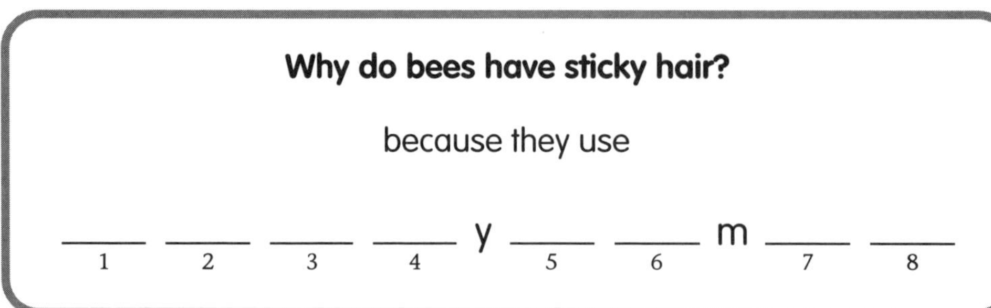

1. watch, cawht, threw

____ ____ ____ ____ ____ ____
  5

2. wunted, fault, water

____ ____ ____ ____ ____ ____
          3

3. walk, wonce, one

____ ____ ____ ____
  2

4. oneder, walk, threw

____ ____ ____ ____ ____ ____
              4

5. work, through, becuz

____ ____ ____ ____ ____ ____ ____
  7   8

6. tawt, watch, wonder

____ ____ ____ ____ ____ ____
              1

7. wonderful, thoughtless, throuh

____ ____ ____ ____ ____ ____ ____
              6

Name ____________________

Secret Code

Use the code of shapes to write each word.

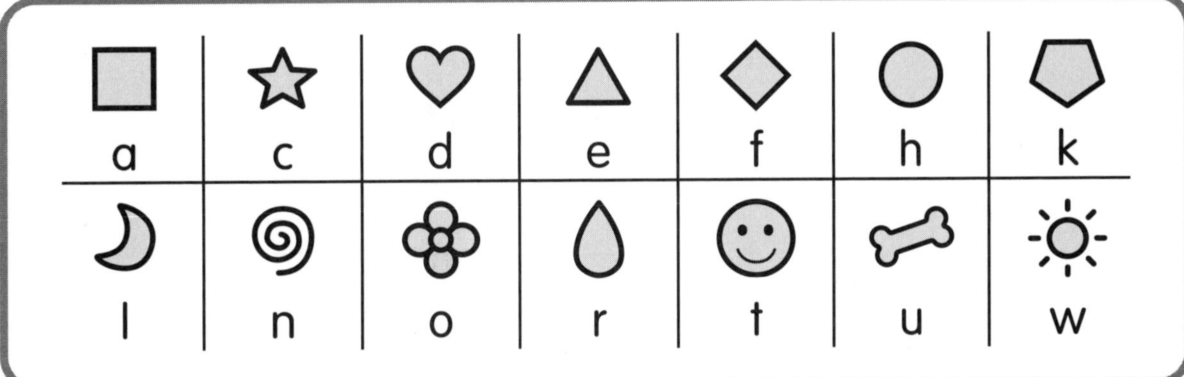

_____ _____ _____ _____ _____

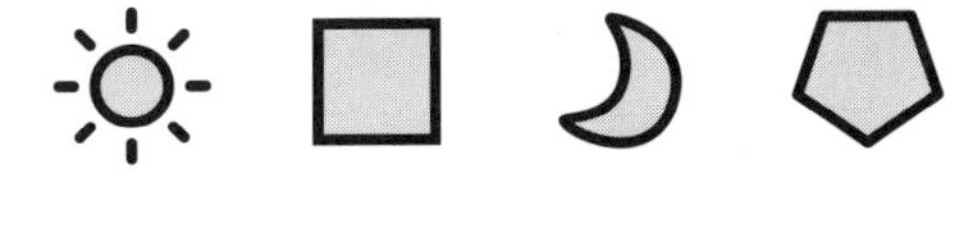

_____ _____ _____ _____

_____ _____ _____ _____ _____

_____ _____ _____ _____ _____

_____ _____ _____ _____ _____

_____ _____ _____

_____ _____ _____ _____ _____ _____ _____ _____ _____

Name ______________________

Three's a Crowd

Only two aliens can ride in each rocket. Cross out the alien that has
a misspelled word. Then write the word correctly on the line.

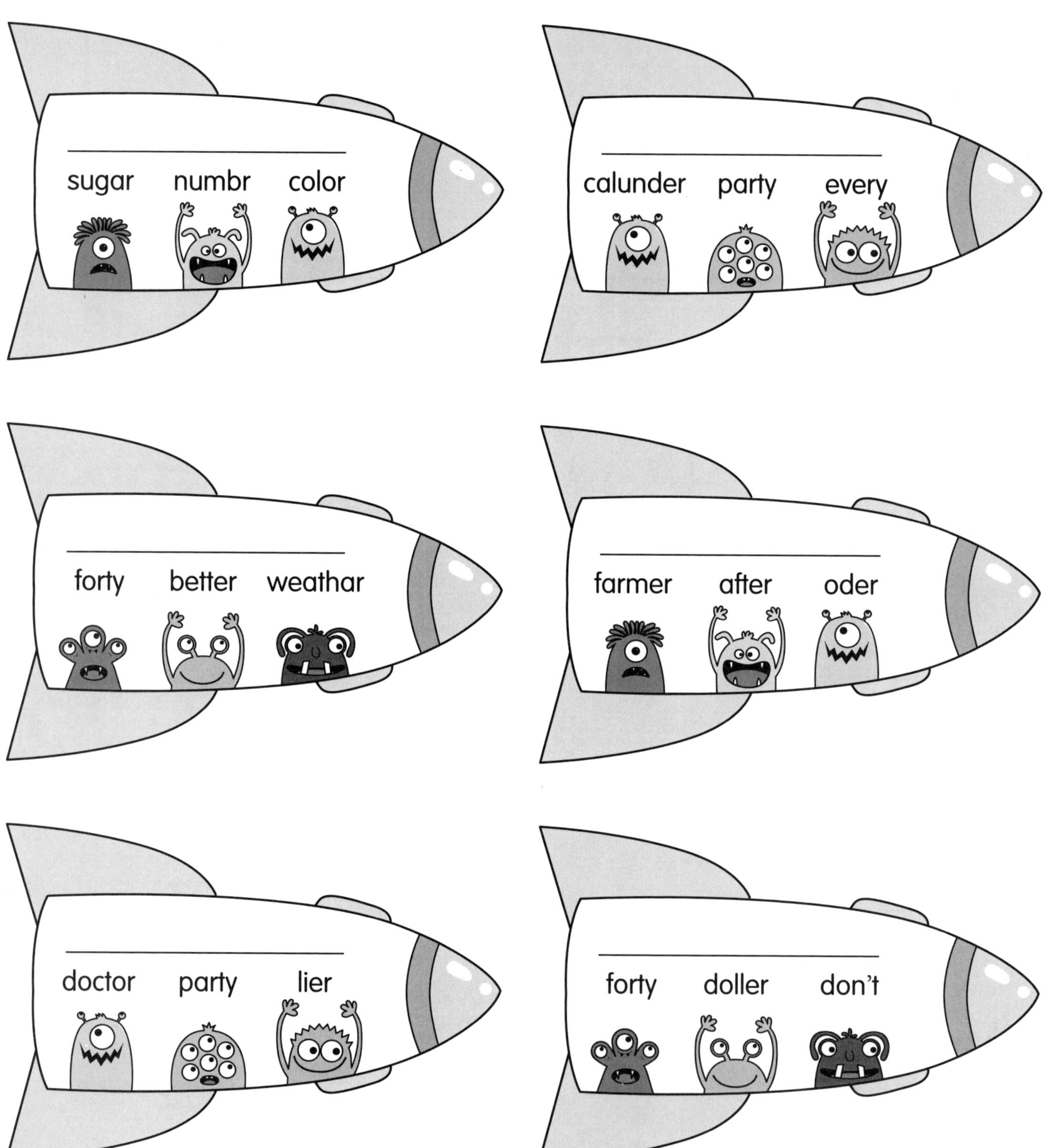

Name _______________________

Animal Barn

Write the letters **ar**, **er**, or **or** to finish spelling the word.
Then draw a line to put the animal in the correct barn.

1.  sug____

2.  col____

3.  p____ty

4.  aft____

5.  bett____

6.  doct____

7.  f____ty

8.  ev____y

9.  f____mer

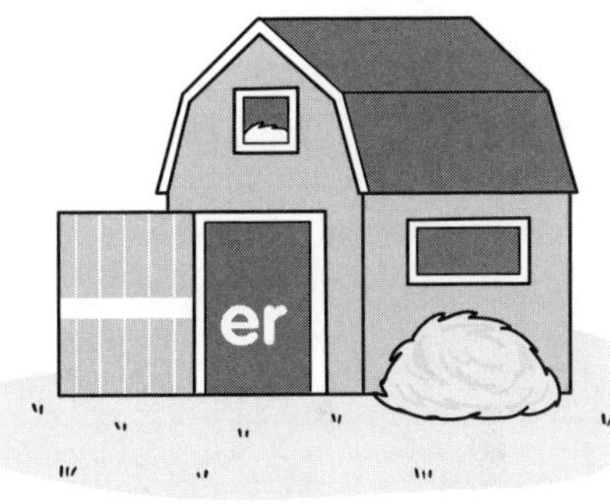

Name ______________________

Sounds Like Fun!

Circle 10 words in the word search that have an **f** sound. The sound can be spelled with an **f**, a **ph**, or a **gh**. Words may go forward, backward, up, down, or diagonally.

alphabet	cough	enough	father	Friday
half	nephew	orphan	phone	photograph

R	I	G	H	T	P	H	O	I	S	F	D	O	G	I	
H	U	N	E	P	H	E	W	U	L	R	E	I	C	G	
A	B	O	S	P	O	I	L	A	O	B	E	S	A	H	
L	A	U	R	N	N	F	H	E	W	O	N	C	L	R	
P	P	V	P	A	E	W	O	L	L	G	H	A	S	T	
H	H	M	P	H	R	I	D	A	Y	P	U	U	W	S	
D	O	A	Y	P	E	T	E	B	A	H	P	L	A	E	
H	T	W	S	R	G	A	O	S	B	A	L	E	C	P	
U	O	M	T	O	I	R	S	U	V	T	L	N	O	H	
F	G	L	E	A	L	F	A	B	E	H	I	A	R	O	
O	R	O	R	T	U	I	T	G	U	E	H	N	E	T	
I	A	N	G	W	O	C	E	M	H	R	P	O	H	A	
D	P	R	O	R	O	P	L	O	T	A	U	Y	T	G	
N	H	V	P	U	A	Y	A	D	I	R	F	T	A	R	
O	Y	R	G	A	E	F	O	N	U	N	A	N	F	A	
U	B	H	U	F	O	T	O	G	R	A	T	H	R	G	
E	H	O	Y	A	E	N	O	U	G	H	R	Y	W	H	

Name ___________________

Spelling Competition

Read each word. Decide what different sounds or word parts the word has.
Use the chart to find out how many points each one gets. Write each word's score.

Sound or Word Part	Points
long e sound spelled with **y**	1
f sound spelled with **ph**	2
f sound spelled with **gh**	3
prefix	4
suffix	5

1. happily   **Score** ______

2. graph   **Score** ______

3. cough   **Score** ______

4. Friday   **Score** ______

5. happiness   **Score** ______

6. orphan   **Score** ______

7. unhappy   **Score** ______

8. enough   **Score** ______

9. happier   **Score** ______

Name _______________________

Seeing Double

Draw a line to match the first and second halves of each word
to make a whole pair of binoculars. Write the word on the line.

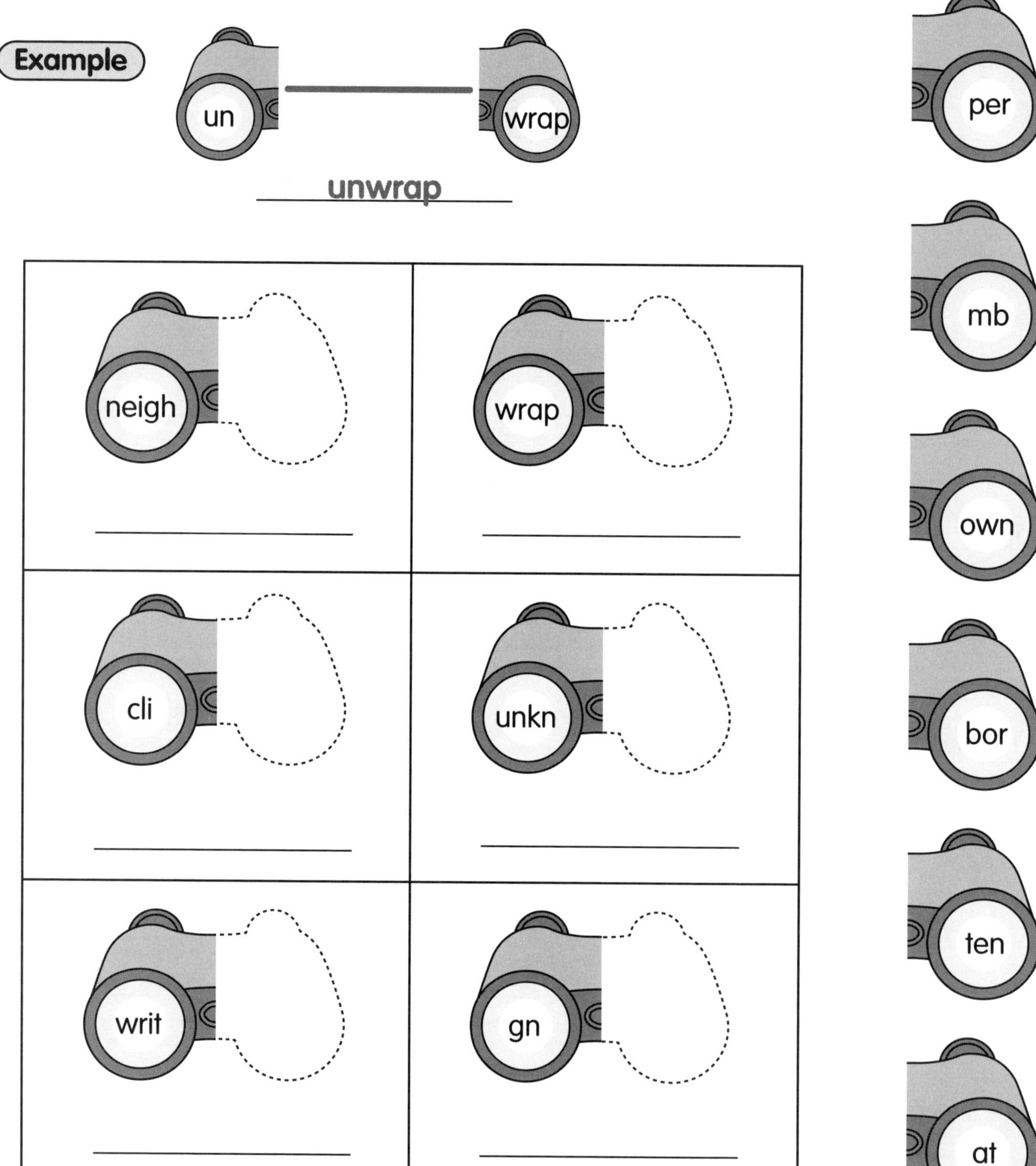

Name _______________________

Crossroads

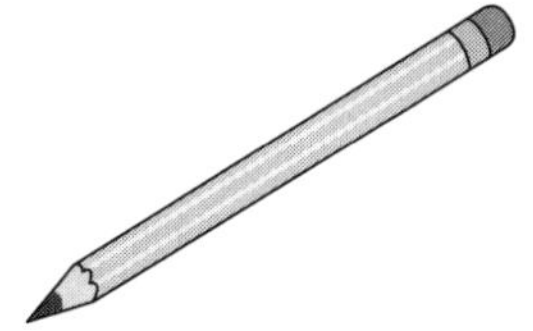

Write each of these words in pairs that share a letter.
Cross out each word as you use it.

climb   ghost   gnat   gnaw   high

~~knew~~   knot   limb   ~~rewrap~~   wrong

Example

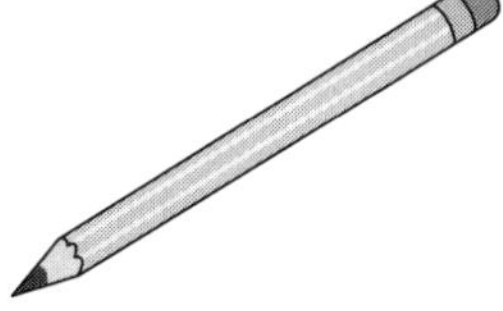

1.

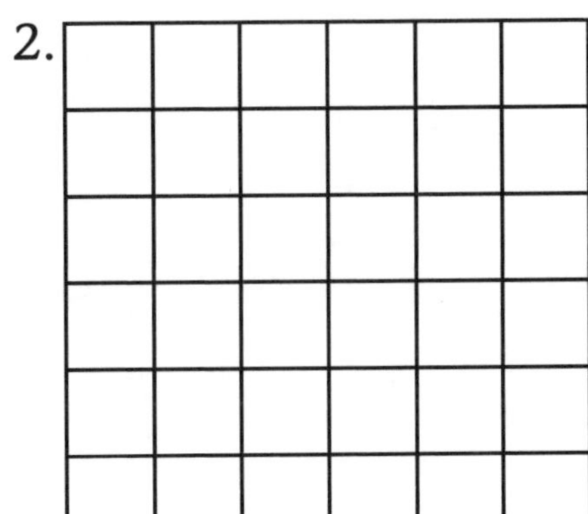

2.

3.

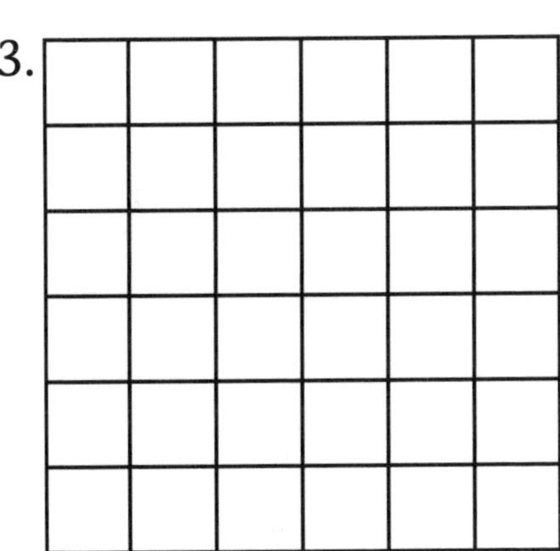

4.

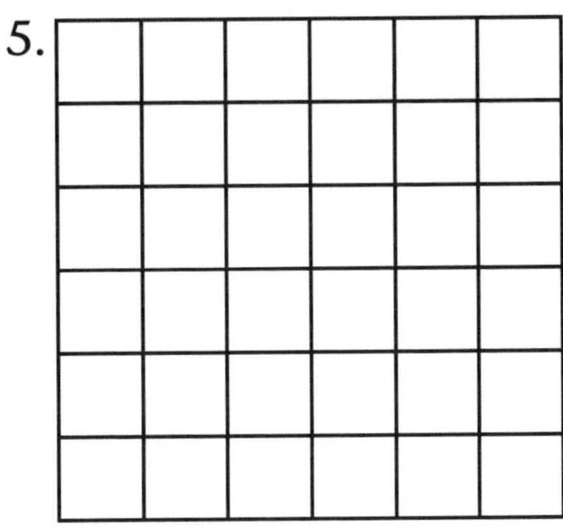

5.

6.

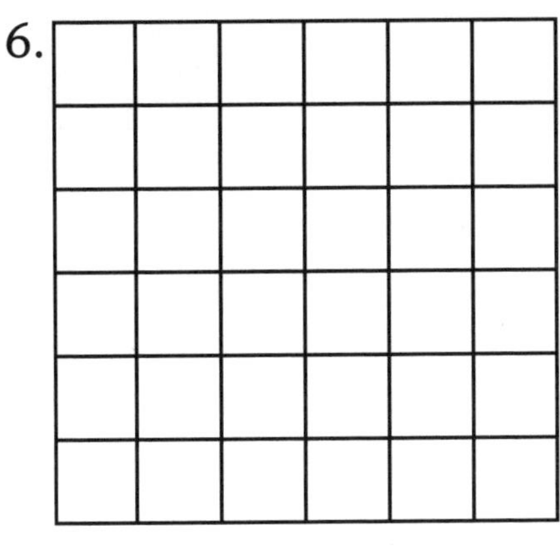

Name ______________________

Opposites Attract

Write the letters **ful**, **ly**, or **less** to write a word next to the left magnet. Then, next to the right magnet, write a word from the box that means the opposite of the first word you wrote.

> careful   careless   fearful   fearless   quickly   slowly   useful   useless

Example

loud __ly__ 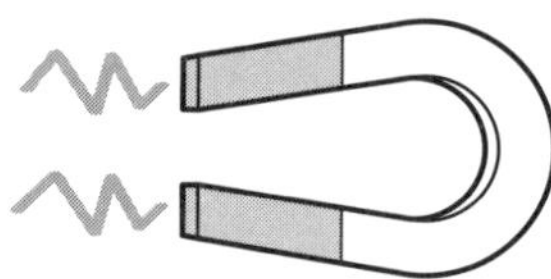 __quietly__

1. quick _______  _______

2. fear _______ 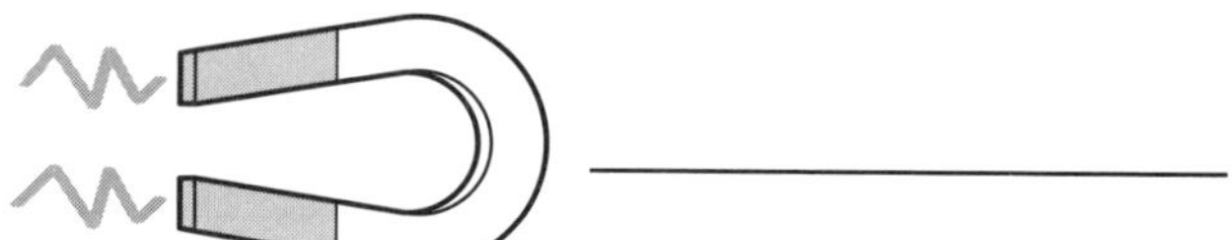 _______

3. care _______ _______

4. use _______ 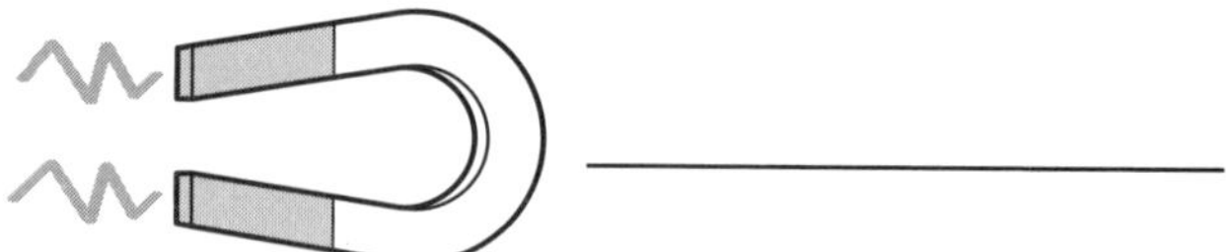 _______

Scrambled Words

Unscramble the letters on each scrambled egg to spell a word from the box.

| fastest | funniest | happiest | joyful | smarter | worthless |

1. 

____

2. 

____

3. 

____

4. 

____

5. 

____

6. 

____

Name _______________________________

Rhyme Time

Write a word from the box to finish the rhyme.

another	early	friend	friendly
heard	measure	shield	year

1. If you give a cookie to my brother,

   he will soon want _____________________.

2. The knight in the field
   was protected by his _____________________.

3. All my family from far and near

   gets together once a _____________________.

4. Have you ever _____________________
   such a silly sound from a bird?

5. I will always lend
   anything to my _____________________.

6. Let's take my picture _____________________
   while my hair is still curly!

Name _______________________

What Word Am I?

Write a spelling word to solve each riddle.

another	break	eat	field	friend
head	measure	mother	shield	year

1. I have a **short e** sound. I'm a body part.

   ____

2. I have a **short u** sound. I am part of a family.

   ____

3. I have a **long e** sound. Sometimes I'm filled with grass and flowers.

   ____

4. I have a **long a** sound. I start with a consonant blend.

   ____

5. I have a **short e** sound. You do this to find out how big something is.

   ____

6. I have a **long e** sound. You do this when you are hungry.

   ____

Name _______________________

Clues to Choose

Read each clue and choose a spelling word to answer it.
Then use the letters in the gray boxes to solve the riddle below.

hour	our	knight	night	soup
peace	piece	their	there	they're
wait	weight	right	write	wrote

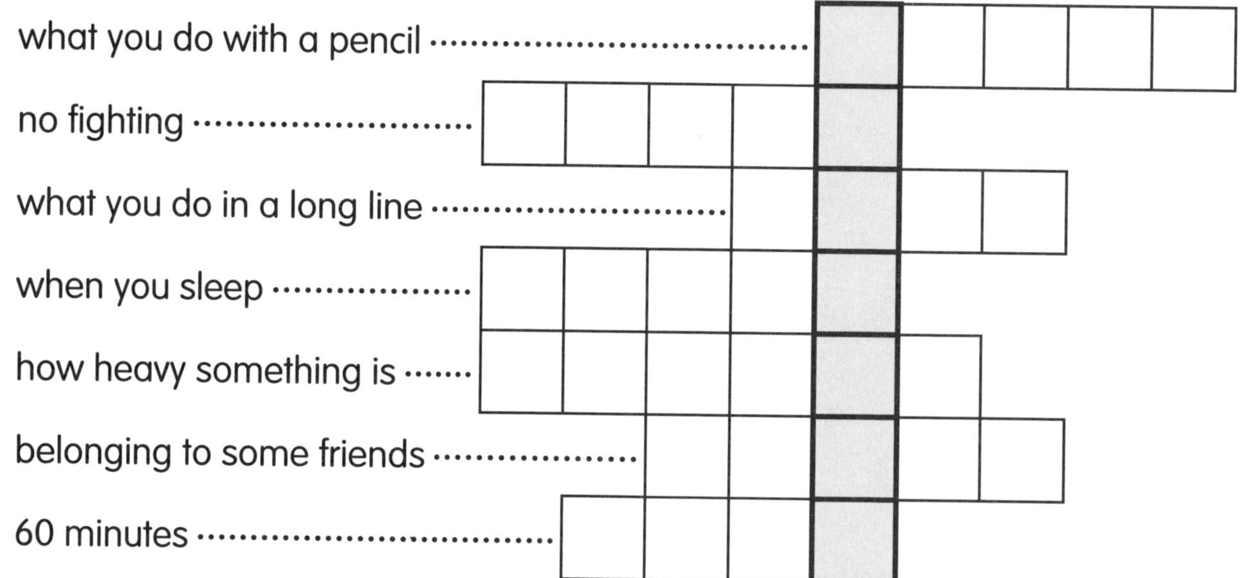

what you do with a pencil ....

no fighting ....

what you do in a long line ....

when you sleep ....

how heavy something is ....

belonging to some friends ....

60 minutes ....

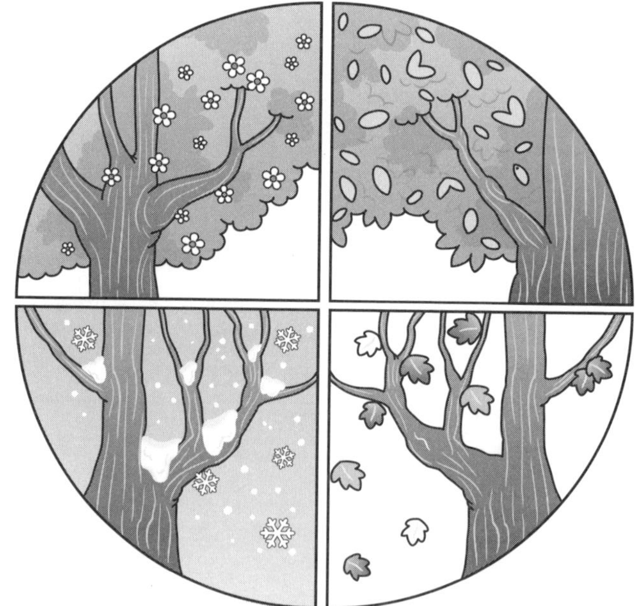

Whether you like winter, spring, summer, or fall, I make it the best season of all!

What am I? _______________________

Ant or Aunt?

Ant and his aunt brought home food to eat. But they don't remember which apples
belong to Ant or his aunt! Look at the spelling words chart. Write a word to finish
each sentence. Then circle Ant or his aunt to show whose apple it is.

	there	night	write	weight	piece	our
	their	knight	right	wait	peace	hour

Name ______________________

Spelling Puzzle

Cut apart the puzzle pieces. Use them to complete page 151.

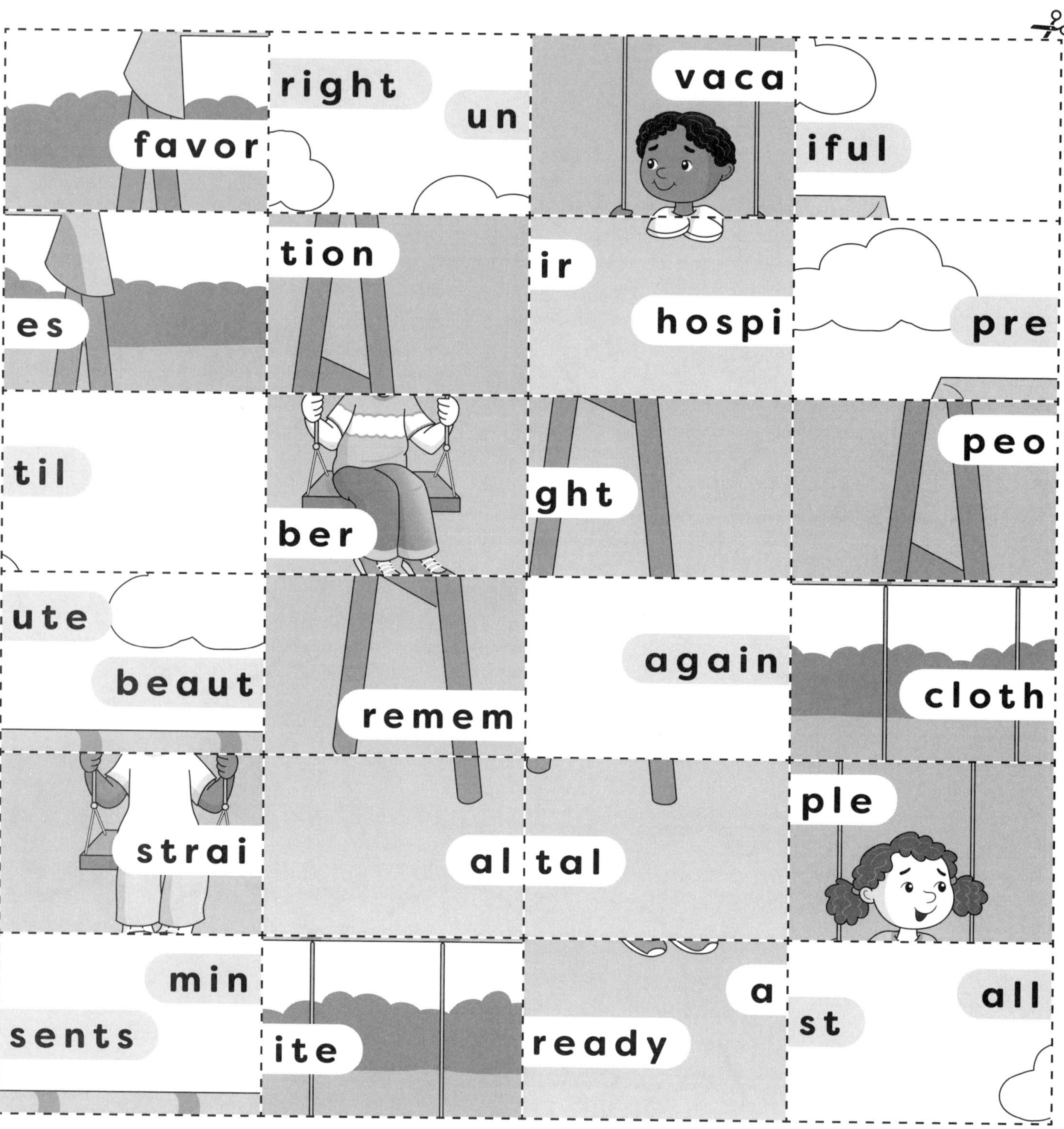

Name _______________________

Spelling Puzzle, *continued*

Put the puzzle pieces together to make spelling words. Then move them to make a picture of a playground. Glue them together below.

glue	glue	glue	glue
glue	glue	glue	glue
glue	glue	glue	glue
glue	glue	glue	glue
glue	glue	glue	glue
glue	glue	glue	glue

How to Spell Hard Words

There are so many words that it would be hard to memorize them all!
It helps to have a plan when you are writing. Here are ways to figure out
how to spell words that you don't know.

	Say the word. Listen to the sounds and syllables. (Ask yourself) What do I hear? What do I know?
i before e except after c	**Think about rules or patterns** using the sounds you heard. (Ask yourself) Is there a rule or pattern I can follow?
-ink family drink link mink pink rink sink think wink	**Think about similar words** that you know how to spell. (Ask yourself) Does it rhyme with another word? Is it part of a word family?
under|stand|ing	**Divide the word.** Break compound words into two parts. Divide between prefix, base word, and suffix. Divide it into syllables. (Ask yourself) How can I divide it into smaller pieces?
success sŭk sĕs´ **to do well**	**Try to spell the word.** You can try different ways. (Ask yourself) Does it look right? Is it in the dictionary?

Spelling Vowel Sounds

Every word has a vowel sound. There are different kinds of vowel sounds.
Look at the chart to find the kind you hear in a word.

I hear a short vowel sound.

Write the letter you hear:

gr**a**ph, h**e**lp, dr**i**nk, s**o**ng,
m**u**ch, s**y**mphony

Or try a digraph:

h**ea**d, fr**ie**nd, t**ou**ch, **aw**ful

I hear a long vowel sound.

Write the letter you hear and
a silent **e** after the consonant:

s**a**ve, th**e**se, pr**i**ce, cl**o**se, c**u**be

Or try a digraph:

br**ea**k, afr**ai**d, tod**ay**, w**eigh**,
pr**ey**, rec**ei**ve, n**ie**ce, **ea**sy,
c**oa**st, thr**ough**, s**ui**t, r**oo**m

I hear a schwa sound.

Any vowel can have a schwa sound:

alive, happ**e**n, tenn**i**s,
o'clock, min**u**te

Make a guess and write the word:
- See if it looks right.
- Check the dictionary.
- Make up a memory clue.

I hear something else.

R-controlled vowels are not
short or long. Write the vowel
that sounds closest.

h**ar**d, p**er**fect, b**ir**d, h**or**se, t**ur**n

Diphthongs are letter pairs that
make two sounds together:

v**oi**ce, l**oy**al, h**ou**se, t**ow**n

Other sounds:

c**oo**k, c**ou**ld, p**u**sh, w**a**tch

Spelling Consonant Sounds

Every word has a consonant sound. Some consonants have two sounds. Look at the chart to find the sound you hear in a word.

 **J** I hear a **j** sound.

Write a **j** most of the time:

enj**o**y, **j**ury

Write a **g** if the next sound is an **e** or **i** sound or if it is the last sound in the word:

dan**ge**r, **gi**ant, chan**ge**

 **S** I hear an **s** sound.

Write an **s** most of the time:

save, al**s**o, **s**urprise, a**s**k, **sl**ow, **sm**ile, **sn**ap

Write a **c** if the next sound is an **e** or **i** sound:

center, re**ci**tal, accura**cy**

 **K** I hear a **k** sound.

Write a **c** most of the time:

carry, be**co**me, **cu**te, **cl**ean, **cr**uise, do**ct**or

Write a **k** if the next sound is an **e** or **i** sound or if it is the last sound in the word:

poc**ke**t, **ki**te, ali**ke**

F I hear an **f** sound.

Write an **f** or **ph** at the beginning:

follow, **ph**one

Write an **f**, **ff**, or **ph** in the middle:

li**f**e, di**ff**erent, al**ph**abet

Write an **f**, **ff**, **ph**, or **gh** at the end:

proo**f**, o**ff**, gra**ph**, cou**gh**

 **?** I hear **something else.**

Digraphs are letter pairs that make a new sound together:

tea**ch**er, **sh**ort, nor**th**, **wh**ere

? What am I **not hearing?**

Many words have **silent letters**. Some are in word families. Memorize them:

clim**b**, co**l**umn, **g**nat, lig**h**t, coul**d**, hal**f**, **h**our, **k**now, **w**rap

Spelling Strategies

Breaking Down Words

It is easier to spell long words when you break them into smaller pieces.

Divide compound words.

Compound words are made of two shorter words put together.

1. Say the word.

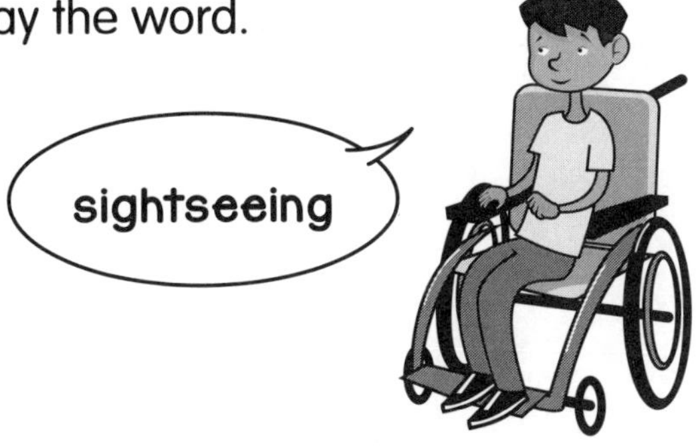

2. Figure out the two words that make up the compound word.

sight

seeing

3. Spell the smaller words.

sightseeing

Divide words between syllables.

Syllables are short pieces of a word. Each syllable has a vowel sound in it. Every time you say a syllable, your chin moves.

1. Say the word.

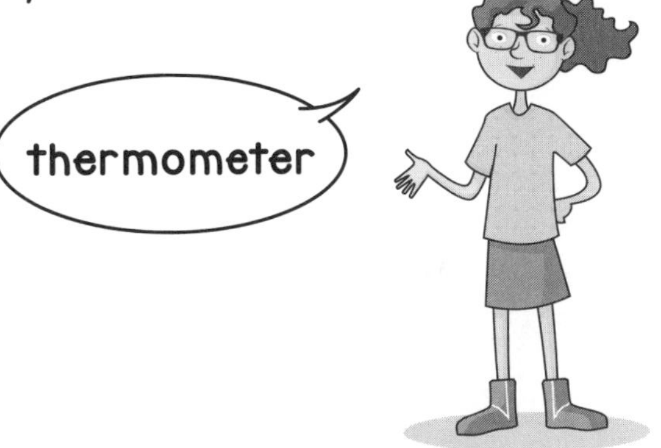

2. Listen to each syllable. Figure out the sounds in each syllable.

ther – mom – e – ter

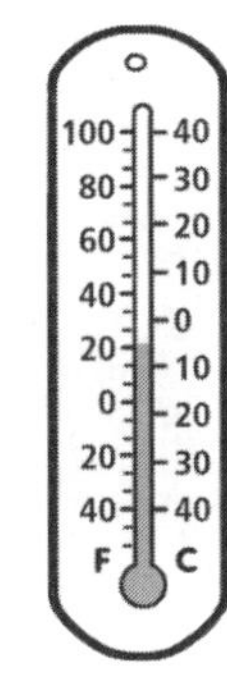

3. Spell the syllables together.

thermometer

Spelling Strategies
Using Suffixes

You can make more words by adding suffixes to the ends of words you know.

Make plural words.

Most nouns: add **s**	Nouns ending in **s**, **ss**, **sh**, **ch**, **x**, or **z**: add **es**	Nouns ending in **y**: drop the **y**, add **ies**
shoe**s**, insect**s**, year**s**	bus**es**, guess**es**, wish**es**, watch**es**, box**es**, waltz**es**	stor**ies**

Make describing words.

Most words: add **er**, **est**, **ly**, **ful**, **ness**, **less**	Words ending in **y**: change **y** to **i** and add the suffix
hard**er**, high**est**, friend**ly**, care**ful**, great**ness**, fear**less**	happ**ier**, happ**iest**, happ**ily**, happ**iness**

Change action words.

Most verbs: add **ed** or **ing**	Verbs ending in **e**: drop the **e** and add **ed** or **ing**	Verbs ending in **y**: change **y** to **i** and add **ed**
finish**ed**, call**ing**	believ**ed**, clos**ing**	carr**ied**

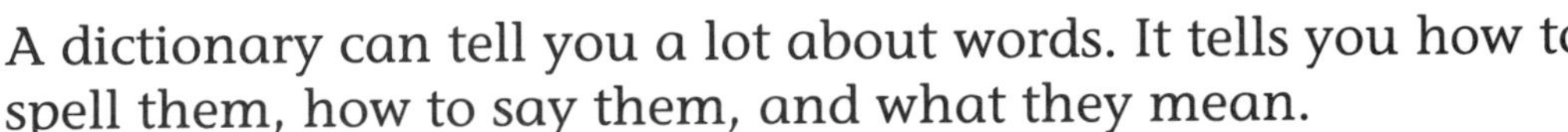

Spelling Strategies
Using a Dictionary

A dictionary can tell you a lot about words. It tells you how to spell them, how to say them, and what they mean.

How to find a word

"I don't know how to spell it. How can I look it up?"

First, guess at the spelling. Is it in the dictionary? If you don't see **howce** there, think of another way to write the **ow** sound. Try **houce**. If you still don't see it, think of another way to write the **soft c** sound. Try **house**.

How to say a word

"I've seen that word before, but what does it sound like?"

After the word is spelled, you'll see symbols that tell you short and long vowels and basic consonant sounds.

It also shows the syllables.

enough (ē nŭf´)

How to learn a word's meanings

"I can read the word, but how do I use it?"

After showing how to say the word, you'll see what it means. If you look up a word that sounds the same as another word, check the meaning to see if you have the right word.

kind (kīnd)

1. nice 2. a type or group

Spelling Strategies
Making Memory Clues

Even if you know every spelling rule, you just have to remember how to spell some words. Making up your own memory clue can be helpful and fun!

Write a rhyming sentence.

This memory clue helps you remember that **climb** has a **silent b** in it.

Be silent and tall as you clim**b** the wall.

Write an acrostic.

The first letter of each word spells **ocean**.

Write a silly sentence.

All the **a**'s remind you that **taught** has an **a** in it.

Annie t**a**ught **a**nts to d**a**nce.

   Spelling Games and Activities • EMC 8273 • © Evan-Moor Corporation

SPELLING IS FUN!
I completed this book!
Name

Answer Key

Page 12

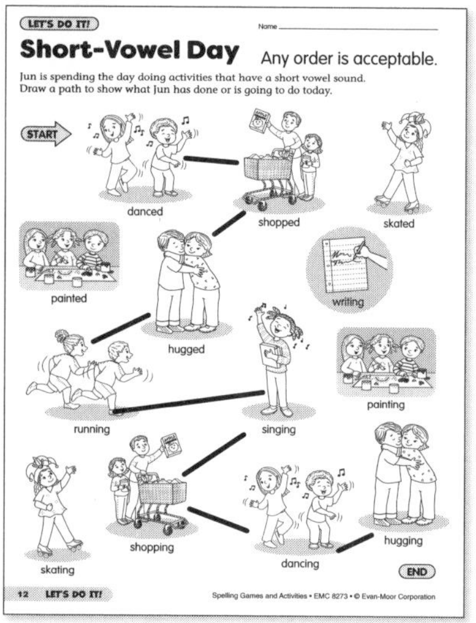

Page 13

Page 14

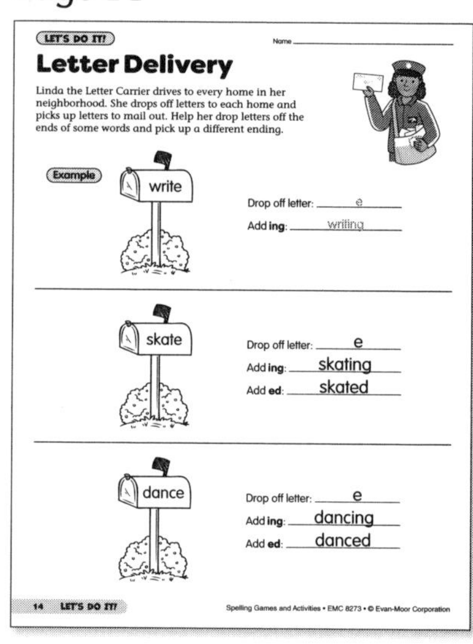

Page 15

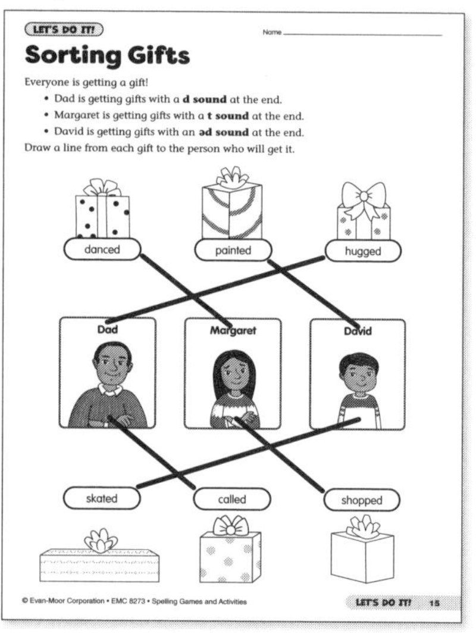

Page 17

Page 18

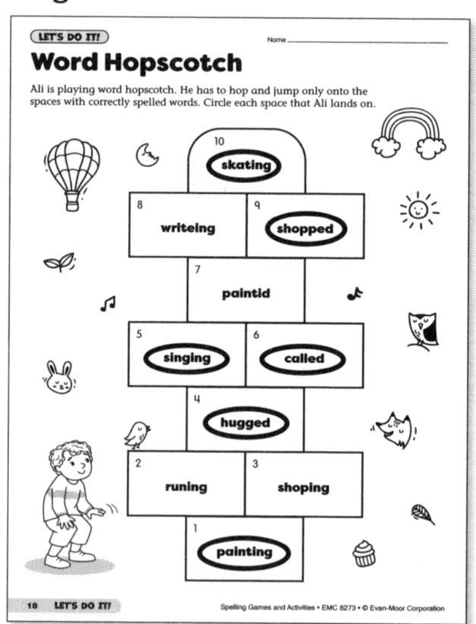

Page 23

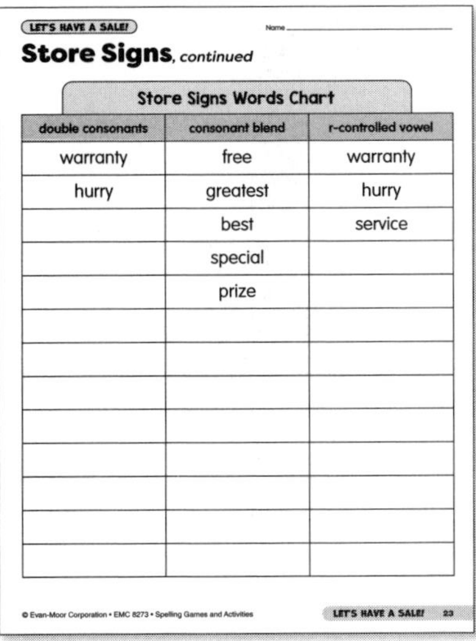

Store Signs, continued

Store Signs Words Chart

double consonants	consonant blend	r-controlled vowel
warranty	free	warranty
hurry	greatest	hurry
	best	service
	special	
	prize	

© Evan-Moor Corporation • EMC 8273 • Spelling Games and Activities — LET'S HAVE A SALE! 23

Page 24

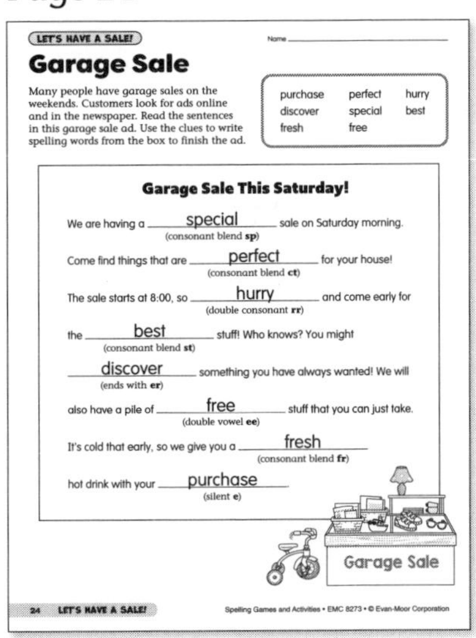

Garage Sale

Many people have garage sales on the weekends. Customers look for ads online and in the newspaper. Read the sentences in this garage sale ad. Use the clues to write spelling words from the box to finish the ad.

purchase   perfect   hurry
discover   special   best
fresh   free

Garage Sale This Saturday!

We are having a __special__ (consonant blend **sp**) sale on Saturday morning.

Come find things that are __perfect__ (consonant blend **ct**) for your house!

The sale starts at 8:00, so __hurry__ (double consonant **rr**) and come early for

the __best__ (consonant blend **st**) stuff! Who knows? You might

__discover__ (ends with **er**) something you have always wanted! We will

also have a pile of __free__ (double vowel **ee**) stuff that you can just take.

It's cold that early, so we give you a __fresh__ (consonant blend **fr**)

hot drink with your __purchase__ (silent **e**)

24 LET'S HAVE A SALE! — Spelling Games and Activities • EMC 8273 • © Evan-Moor Corporation

Page 25

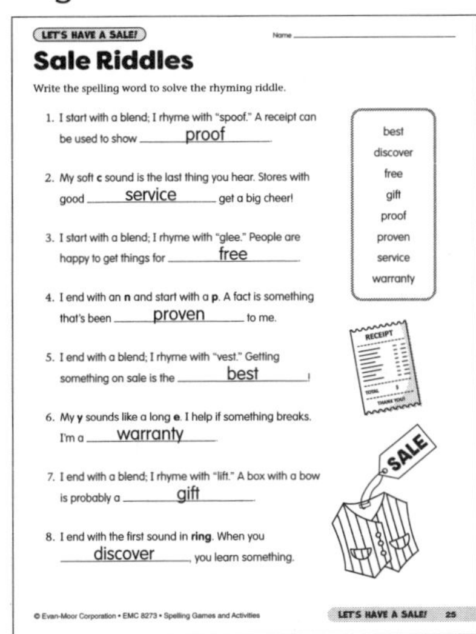

Sale Riddles

Write the spelling word to solve the rhyming riddle.

1. I start with a blend; I rhyme with "spoof." A receipt can be used to show __proof__

2. My soft **c** sound is the last thing you hear. Stores with good __service__ get a big cheer!

3. I start with a blend; I rhyme with "glee." People are happy to get things for __free__

4. I end with an **n** and start with a **p**. A fact is something that's been __proven__ to me.

5. I end with a blend; I rhyme with "vest." Getting something on sale is the __best__!

6. My **y** sounds like a long **e**. I help if something breaks. I'm a __warranty__

7. I end with a blend; I rhyme with "lift." A box with a bow is probably a __gift__

8. I end with the first sound in **ring**. When you __discover__, you learn something.

best
discover
free
gift
proof
proven
service
warranty

© Evan-Moor Corporation • EMC 8273 • Spelling Games and Activities — LET'S HAVE A SALE! 25

Page 26

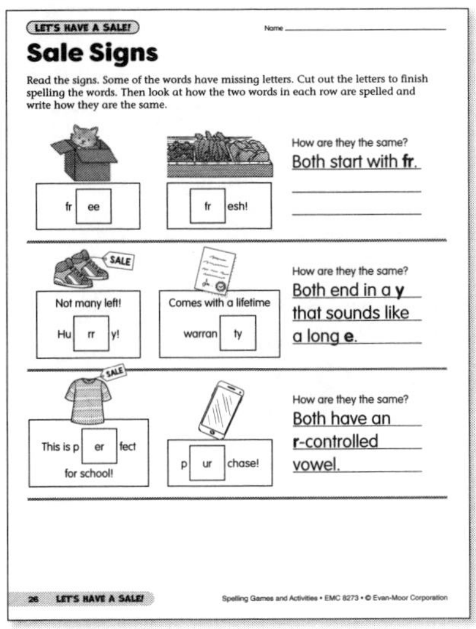

Sale Signs

Read the signs. Some of the words have missing letters. Cut out the letters to finish spelling the words. Then look at how the two words in each row are spelled and write how they are the same.

fr | ee

fr | esh!

How are they the same?
Both start with **fr**.

Not many left! Hu | rr | y!

Comes with a lifetime warran | ty

How are they the same?
Both end in a **y** that sounds like a long **e**.

This is p | er | fect for school!

p | ur | chase!

How are they the same?
Both have an r-controlled vowel.

26 LET'S HAVE A SALE! — Spelling Games and Activities • EMC 8273 • © Evan-Moor Corporation

Page 27

What's the Price?

Samir's Sports Supplies is having a sale, but they forgot to write the prices! Use the word on the tag and the chart to write a price for each item. If a word has more than one price, add them.

Letters and Sounds	Price
Soft c sound	$18.00
Ending blend	$12.00
Long e sound at the end	$24.00
Beginning blend	$10.00

service $ 18.00
gift $ 12.00
proven $ 10.00

prize $ 10.00
hurry $ 24.00
perfect $ 12.00

greatest $ 22.00
proof $ 10.00
special $ 10.00

© Evan-Moor Corporation • EMC 8273 • Spelling Games and Activities — LET'S HAVE A SALE! 27

Page 32

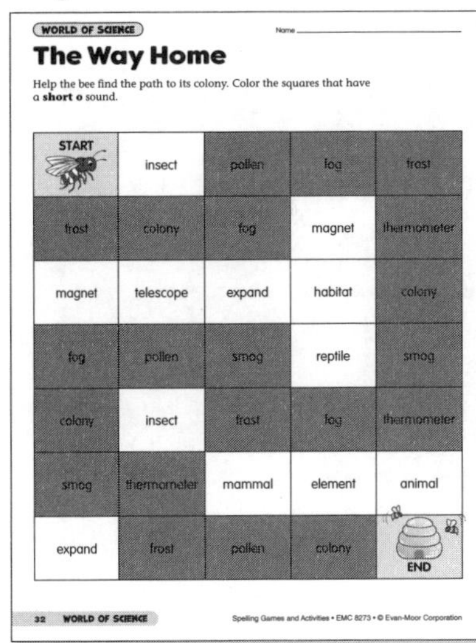

The Way Home

Help the bee find the path to its colony. Color the squares that have a **short o** sound.

START	insect	pollen	fog	frost
frost	colony	fog	magnet	thermometer
magnet	telescope	expand	habitat	colony
fog	pollen	smog	reptile	smog
colony	insect	frost	fog	thermometer
smog	thermometer	mammal	element	animal
expand	frost	pollen	colony	END

32 WORLD OF SCIENCE — Spelling Games and Activities • EMC 8273 • © Evan-Moor Corporation

Page 33

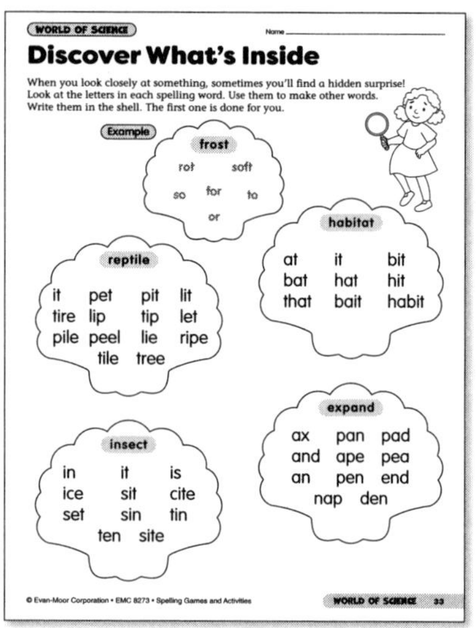

Discover What's Inside

When you look closely at something, sometimes you'll find a hidden surprise!
Look at the letters in each spelling word. Use them to make other words.
Write them in the shell. The first one is done for you.

Example

frost
rot   soft
so   for   to
or

reptile
it   pet   pit   lit
tire   lip   tip   let
pile   peel   lie   ripe
tile   tree

habitat
at   it   bit
bat   hat   hit
that   bait   habit

insect
in   it   is
ice   sit   cite
set   sin   tin
ten   site

expand
ax   pan   pad
and   ape   pea
an   pen   end
nap   den

Page 34

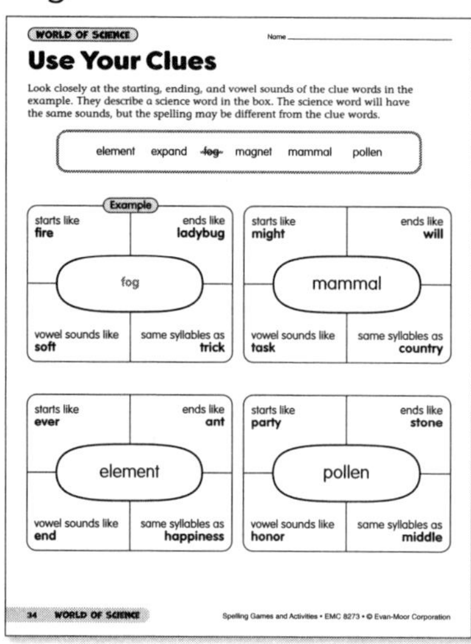

Use Your Clues

Look closely at the starting, ending, and vowel sounds of the clue words in the
example. They describe a science word in the box. The science word will have
the same sounds, but the spelling may be different from the clue words.

element   expand   ~~fog~~   magnet   mammal   pollen

Example

| starts like **fire** | ends like **ladybug** |
| vowel sounds like **soft** | same syllables as **trick** |

fog

| starts like **might** | ends like **will** |
| vowel sounds like **task** | same syllables as **country** |

mammal

| starts like **ever** | ends like **ant** |
| vowel sounds like **end** | same syllables as **happiness** |

element

| starts like **party** | ends like **stone** |
| vowel sounds like **honor** | same syllables as **middle** |

pollen

Page 35

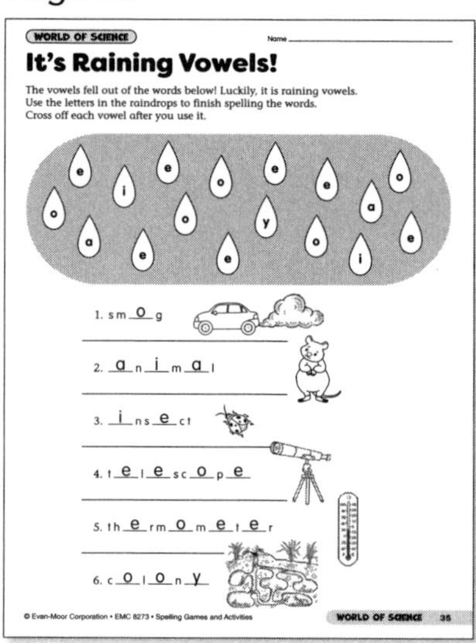

It's Raining Vowels!

The vowels fell out of the words below! Luckily, it is raining vowels.
Use the letters in the raindrops to finish spelling the words.
Cross off each vowel after you use it.

1. s m _O_ g
2. _a_ n _i_ m _a_ l
3. _i_ n s _e_ c t
4. t _e_ l _e_ s c _o_ p e
5. th _e_ r m _o_ m _e_ t _e_ r
6. c _o_ l _o_ n y

Page 36

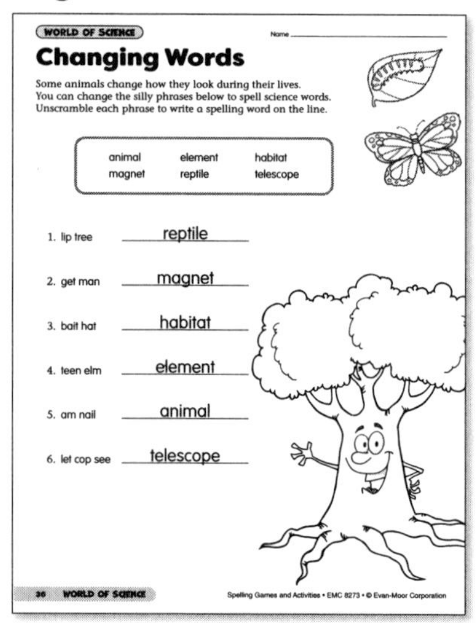

Changing Words

Some animals change how they look during their lives.
You can change the silly phrases below to spell science words.
Unscramble each phrase to write a spelling word on the line.

animal   element   habitat
magnet   reptile   telescope

1. lip tree   reptile
2. get man   magnet
3. bait hat   habitat
4. teen elm   element
5. am nail   animal
6. let cop see   telescope

Page 37

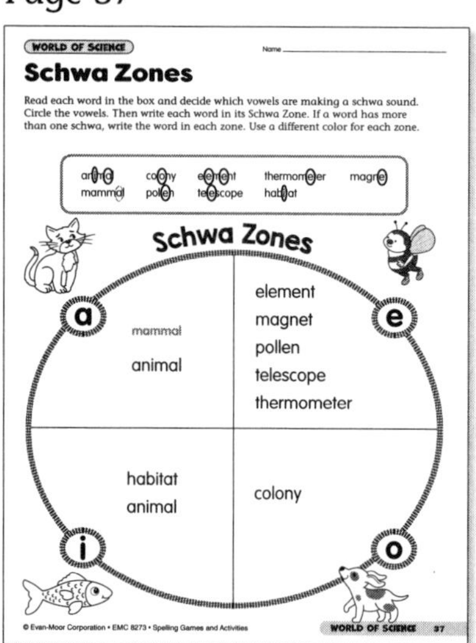

Schwa Zones

Read each word in the box and decide which vowels are making a schwa sound.
Circle the vowels. Then write each word in its Schwa Zone. If a word has more
than one schwa, write the word in each zone. Use a different color for each zone.

anim(a)l   col(o)ny   elem(e)nt   thermom(e)ter   magn(e)t
mamm(a)l   poll(e)n   telescope   hab(i)t(a)t

Schwa Zones

a
mammal
animal

e
element
magnet
pollen
telescope
thermometer

i

o
habitat
animal

colony

Page 42

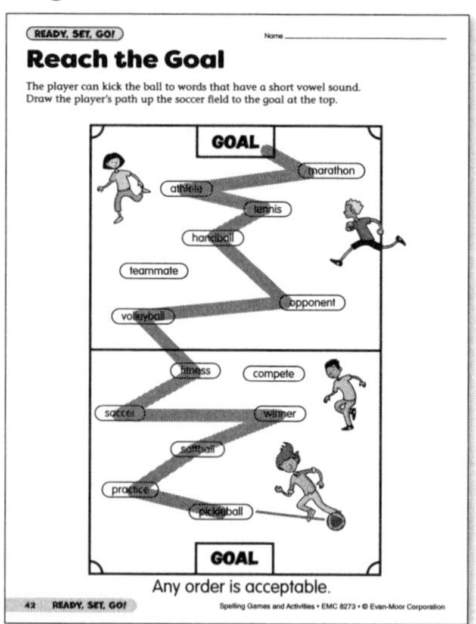

Reach the Goal

The player can kick the ball to words that have a short vowel sound.
Draw the player's path up the soccer field to the goal at the top.

Any order is acceptable.

Spelling Games and Activities • EMC 8273 • © Evan-Moor Corporation

Page 43

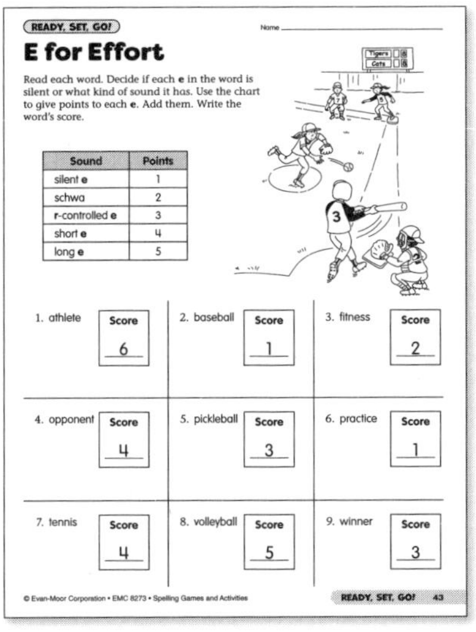

Page 44

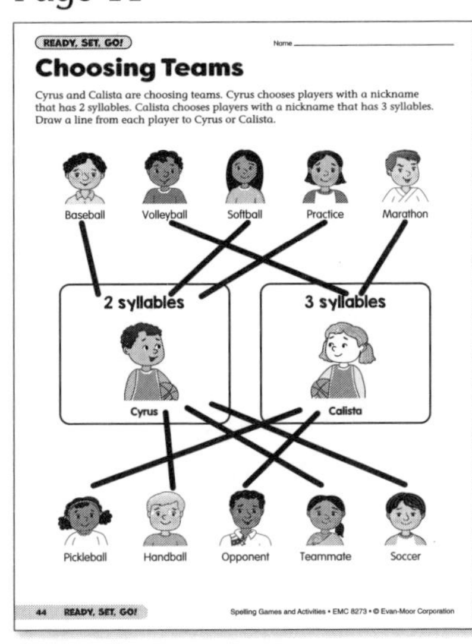

Page 45

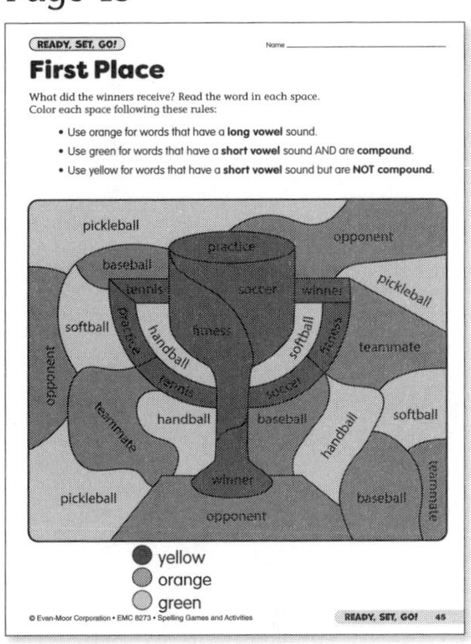

Page 47

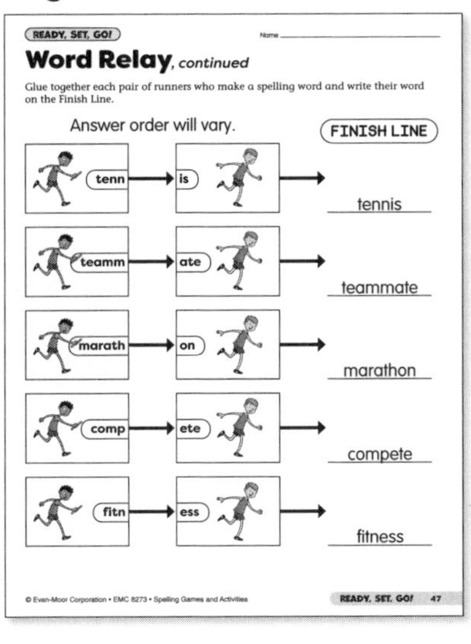

Page 48

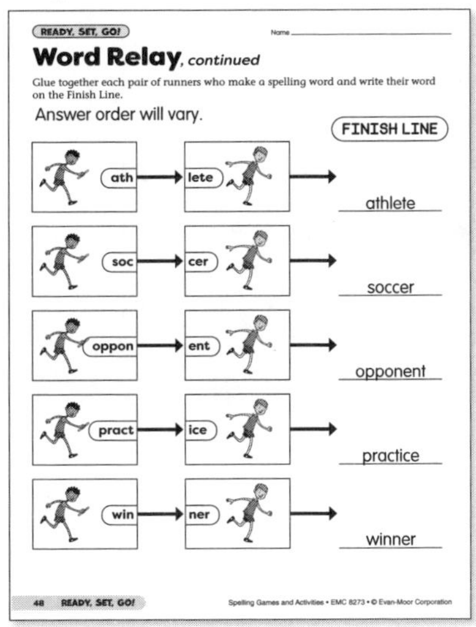

Page 52

Page 53

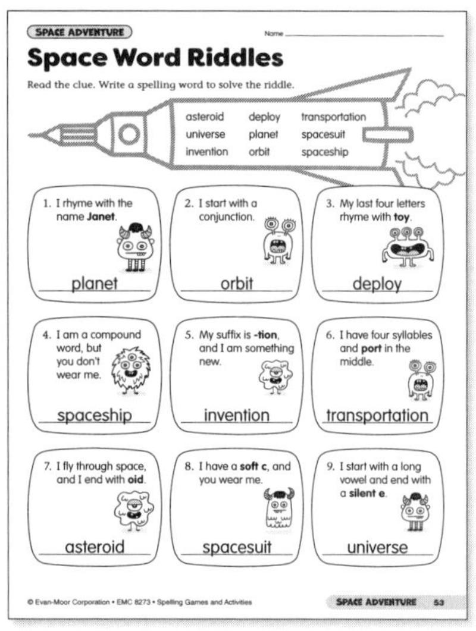

Page 54

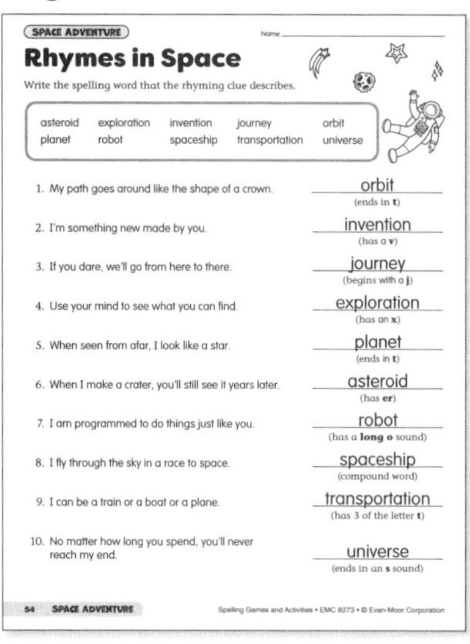

Page 55

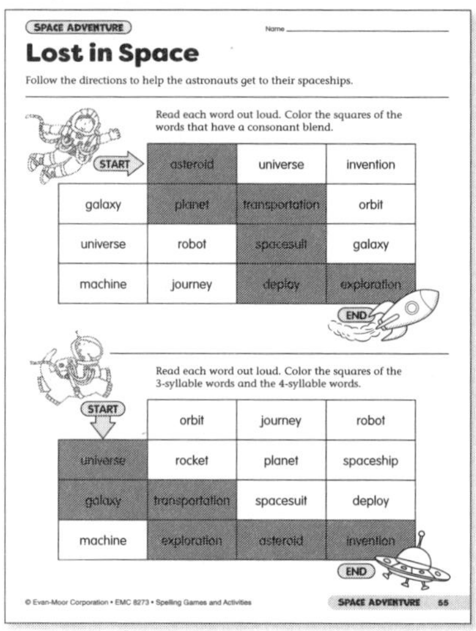

Page 57

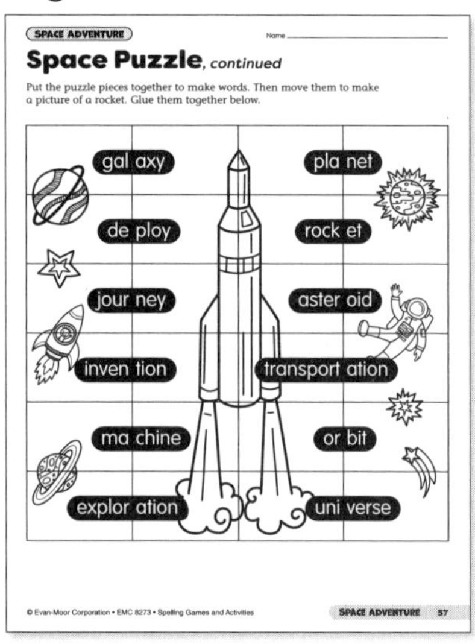

Page 62

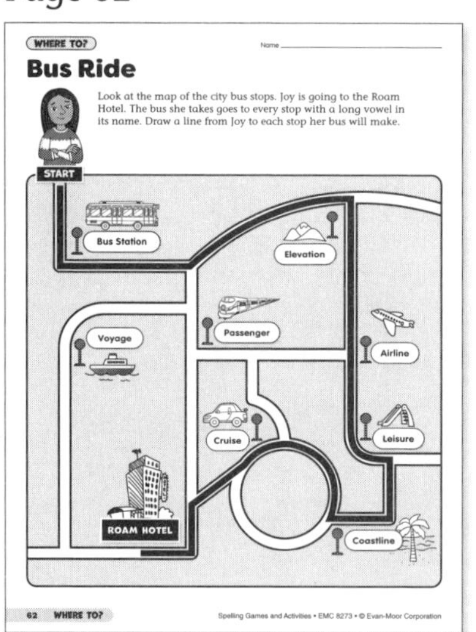

Page 63

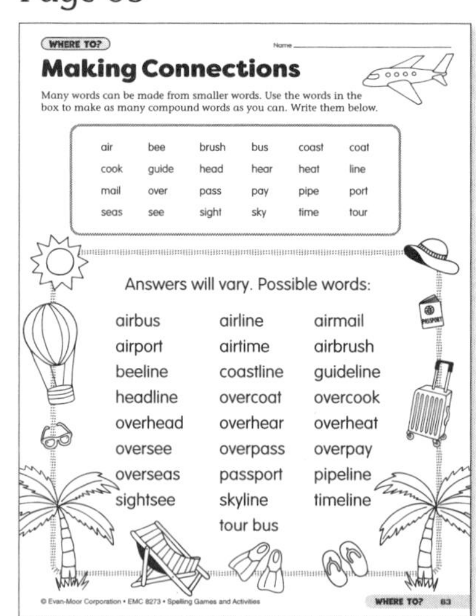

Spelling Games and Activities • EMC 8273 • © Evan-Moor Corporation

Page 64

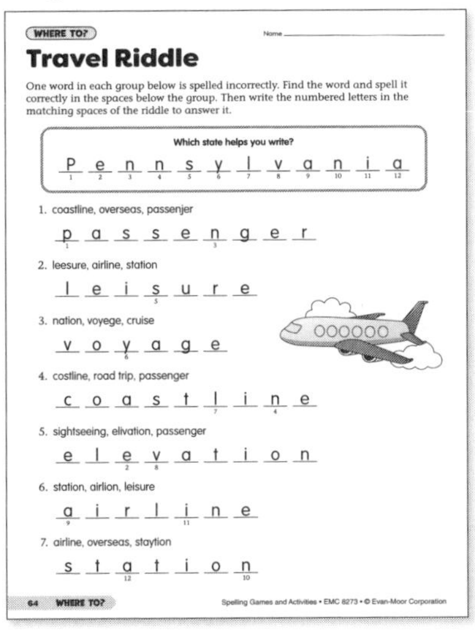

Page 65

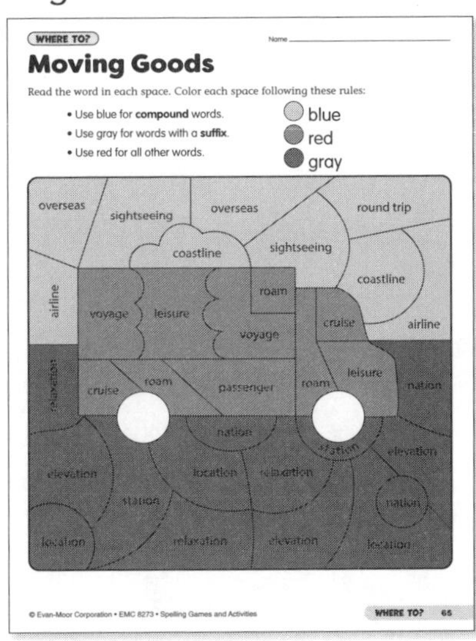

Page 66

Page 72

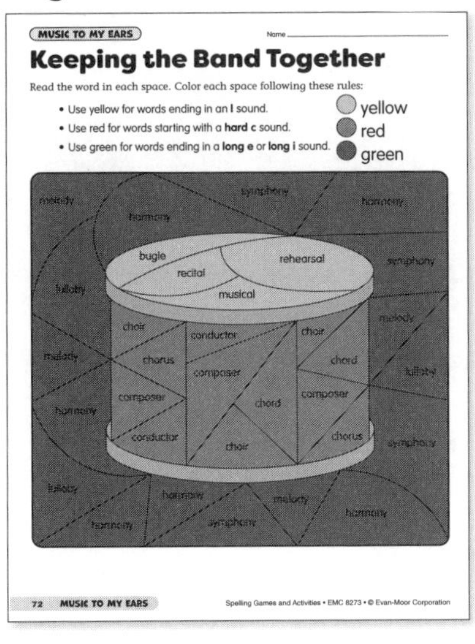

Page 73

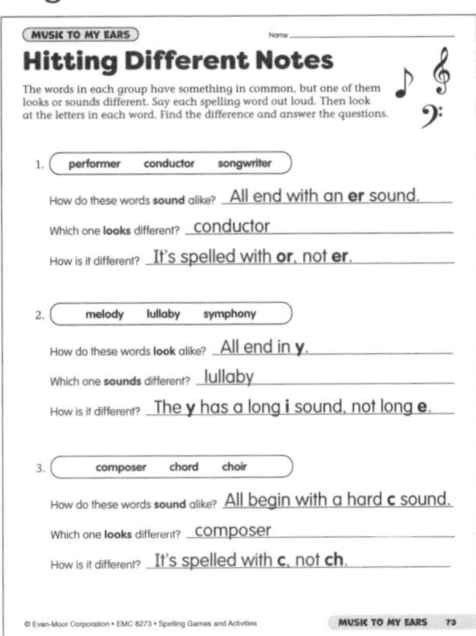

Page 74

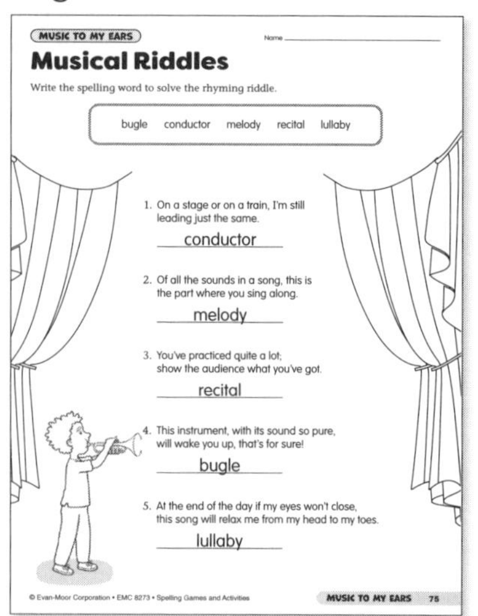

Musical Riddles

Write the spelling word to solve the rhyming riddle.

bugle   conductor   melody   recital   lullaby

1. On a stage or on a train, I'm still leading just the same.
   conductor

2. Of all the sounds in a song, this is the part where you sing along.
   melody

3. You've practiced quite a lot; show the audience what you've got.
   recital

4. This instrument, with its sound so pure, will wake you up, that's for sure!
   bugle

5. At the end of the day if my eyes won't close, this song will relax me from my head to my toes.
   lullaby

© Evan-Moor Corporation • EMC 8273 • Spelling Games and Activities   MUSIC TO MY EARS   75

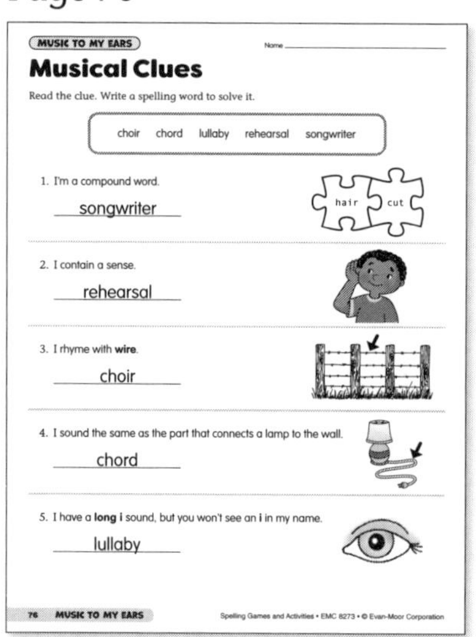

Musical Clues

Read the clue. Write a spelling word to solve it.

choir   chord   lullaby   rehearsal   songwriter

1. I'm a compound word.
   songwriter

2. I contain a sense.
   rehearsal

3. I rhyme with **wire**.
   choir

4. I sound the same as the part that connects a lamp to the wall.
   chord

5. I have a **long i** sound, but you won't see an **i** in my name.
   lullaby

76   MUSIC TO MY EARS   Spelling Games and Activities • EMC 8273 • © Evan-Moor Corporation

Edit My Song

Misspelling a word is like singing a wrong note in a song. Read the song. Five of the words are misspelled. Circle them and write them correctly on the lines below.

Song of the Shore

symphony   recital   performers
chorus   harmony

© Evan-Moor Corporation • EMC 8273 • Spelling Games and Activities   MUSIC TO MY EARS   77

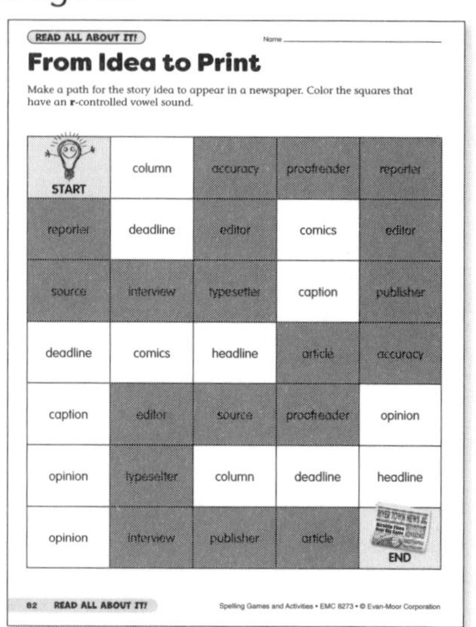

From Idea to Print

Make a path for the story idea to appear in a newspaper. Color the squares that have an **r**-controlled vowel sound.

START	column	accuracy	proofreader	reporter
reporter	deadline	editor	comics	editor
source	interview	typesetter	caption	publisher
deadline	comics	headline	article	accuracy
caption	editor	source	proofreader	opinion
opinion	typesetter	column	deadline	headline
opinion	interview	publisher	article	END

82   READ ALL ABOUT IT!   Spelling Games and Activities • EMC 8273 • © Evan-Moor Corporation

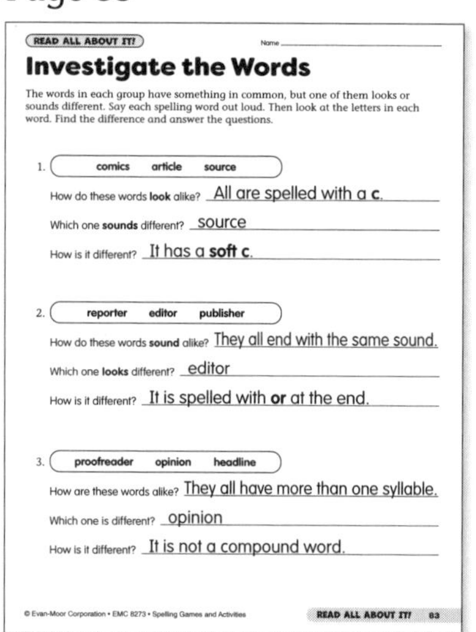

Investigate the Words

The words in each group have something in common, but one of them looks or sounds different. Say each spelling word out loud. Then look at the letters in each word. Find the difference and answer the questions.

1. comics   article   source
   How do these words **look** alike? All are spelled with a **c**.
   Which one **sounds** different? source
   How is it different? It has a **soft c**.

2. reporter   editor   publisher
   How do these words **sound** alike? They all end with the same sound.
   Which one **looks** different? editor
   How is it different? It is spelled with **or** at the end.

3. proofreader   opinion   headline
   How are these words alike? They all have more than one syllable.
   Which one is different? opinion
   How is it different? It is not a compound word.

© Evan-Moor Corporation • EMC 8273 • Spelling Games and Activities   READ ALL ABOUT IT!   83

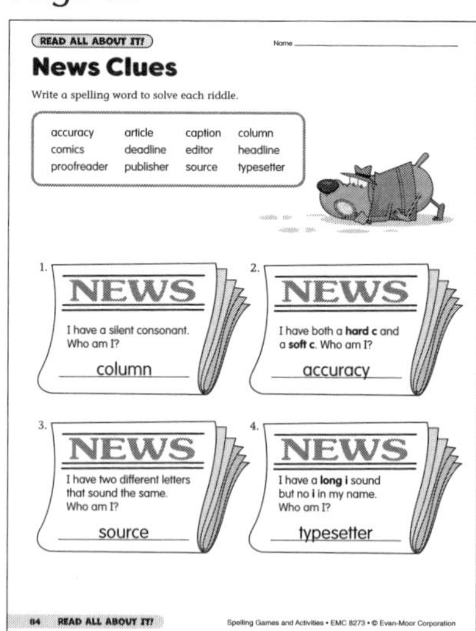

News Clues

Write a spelling word to solve each riddle.

accuracy   article   caption   column
comics   deadline   editor   headline
proofreader   publisher   source   typesetter

1. **NEWS** — I have a silent consonant. Who am I?
   column

2. **NEWS** — I have both a **hard c** and a **soft c**. Who am I?
   accuracy

3. **NEWS** — I have two different letters that sound the same. Who am I?
   source

4. **NEWS** — I have a **long i** sound but no **i** in my name. Who am I?
   typesetter

84   READ ALL ABOUT IT!   Spelling Games and Activities • EMC 8273 • © Evan-Moor Corporation

Page 85

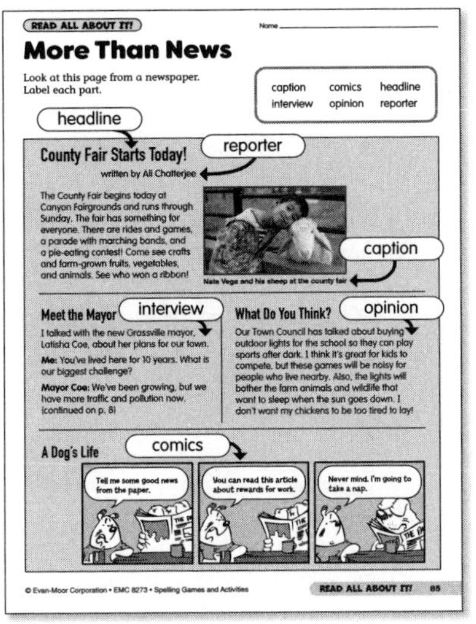

Page 86

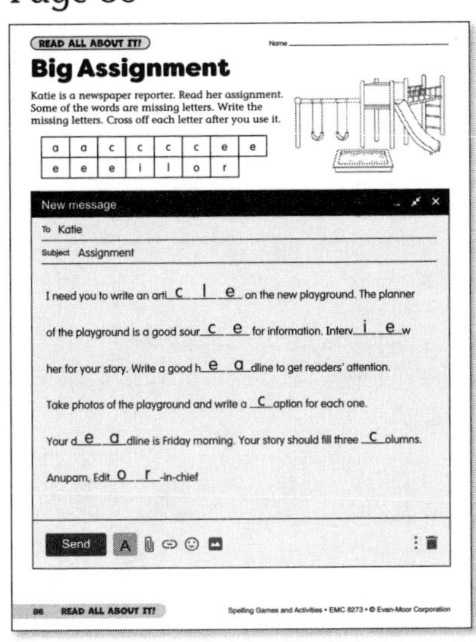

Page 87

Page 92

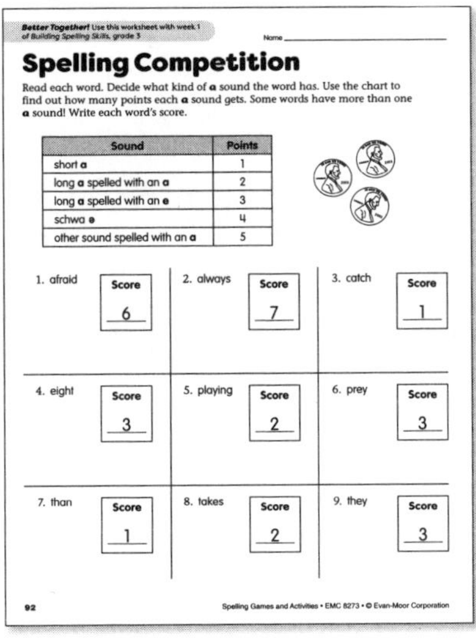

Page 93

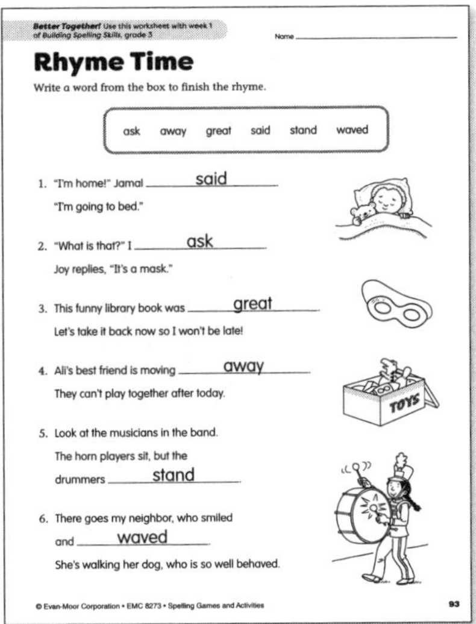

Page 94

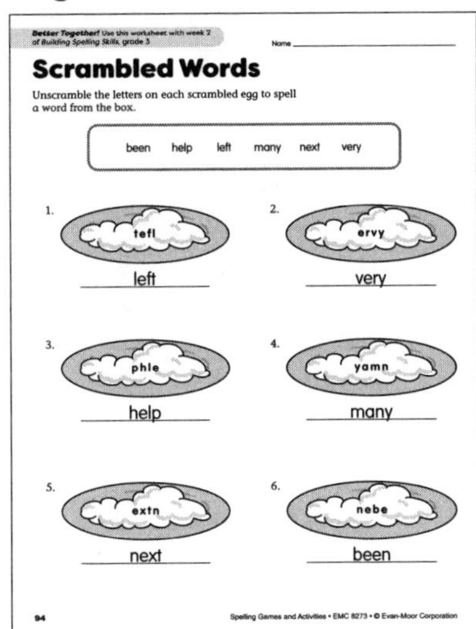

Page 95

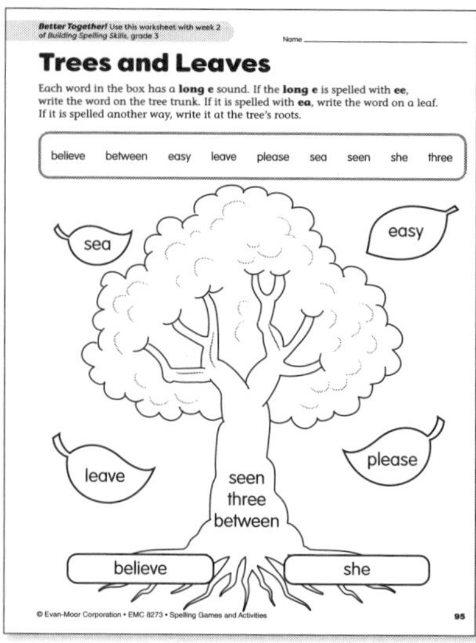

Page 96

Page 97

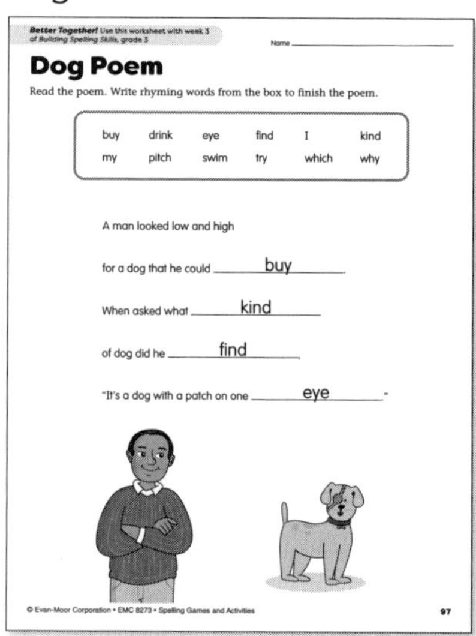

Page 98

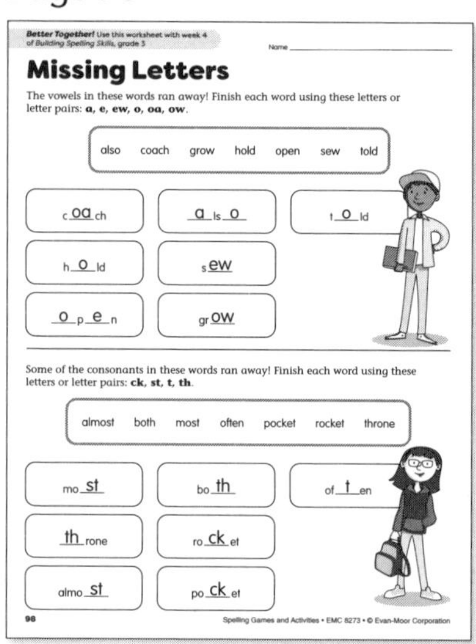

Page 100

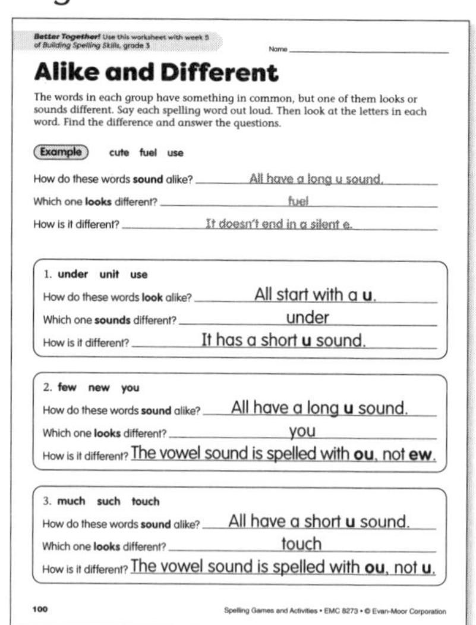

Page 101

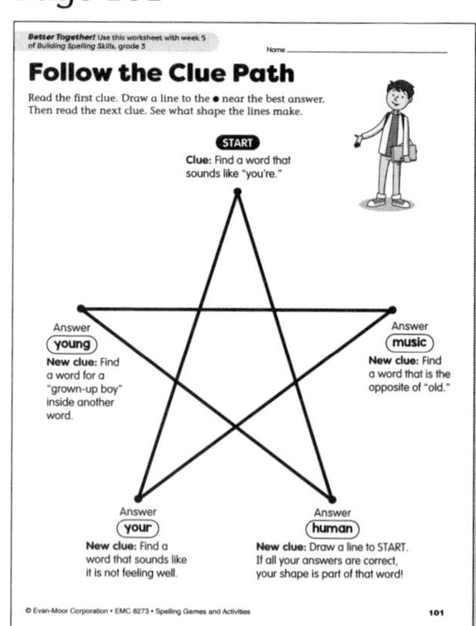

Spelling Games and Activities • EMC 8273 • © Evan-Moor Corporation

Page 102

Page 103

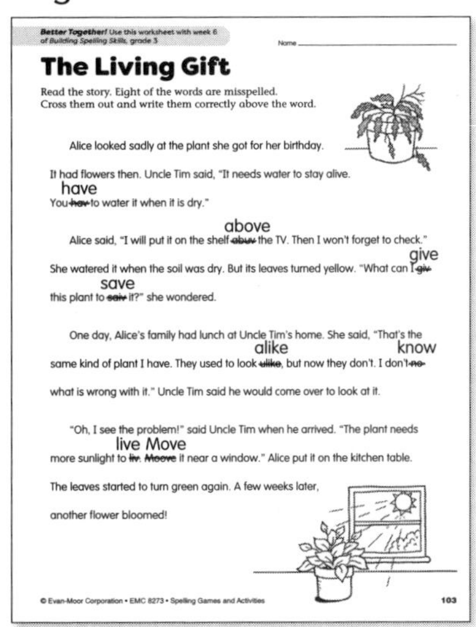

Page 104

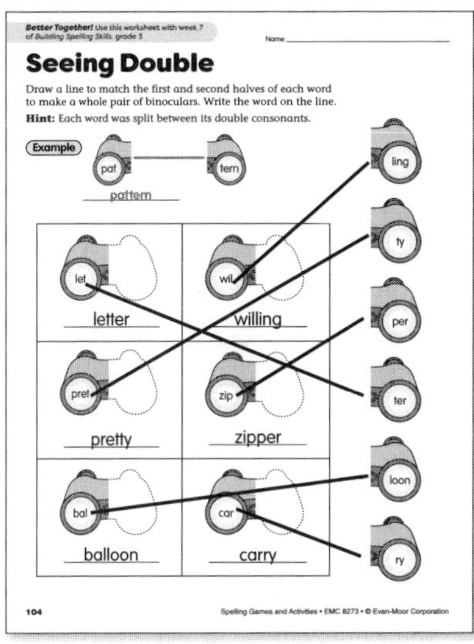

Page 105

Page 106

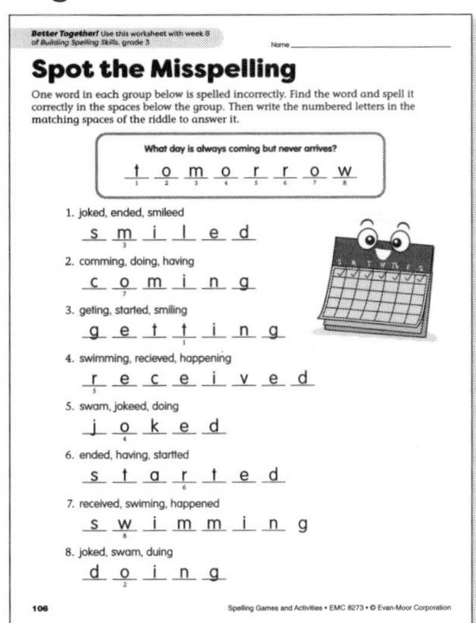

Page 107

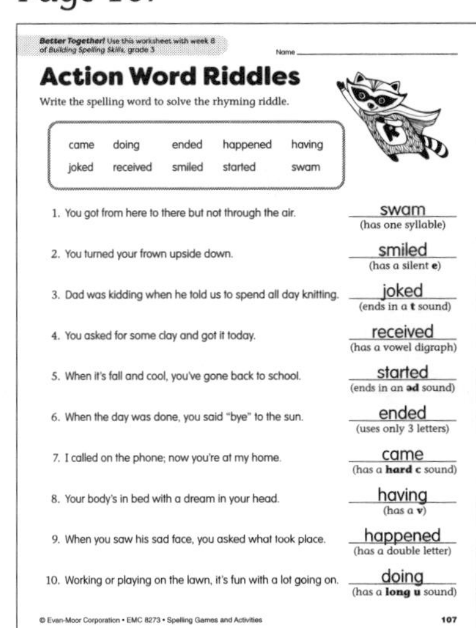

Page 108

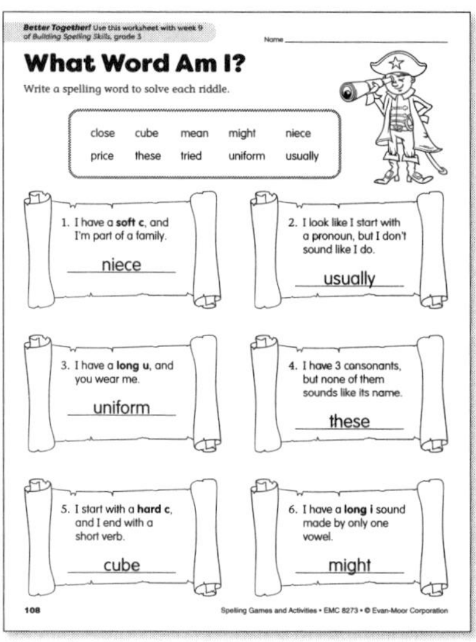

Page 109

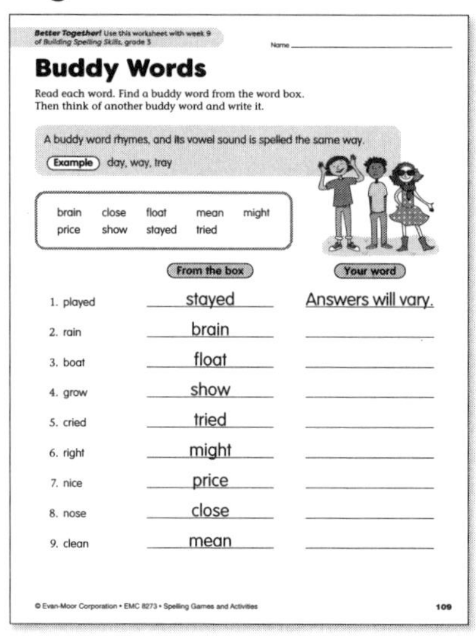

Page 110

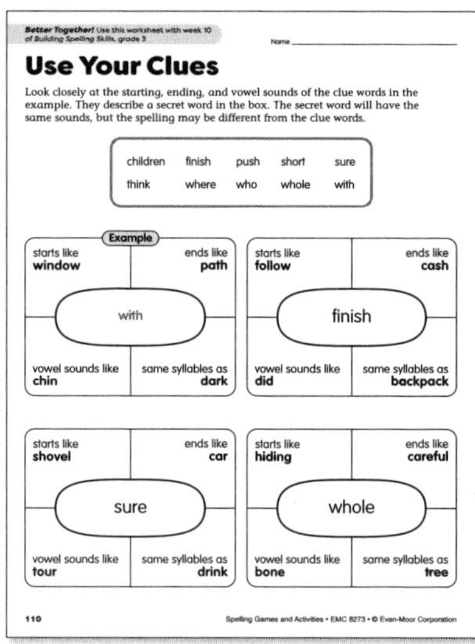

Page 111

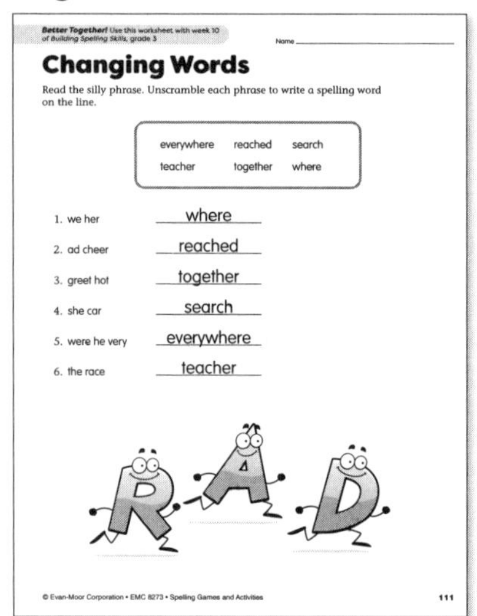

Page 113

Page 114

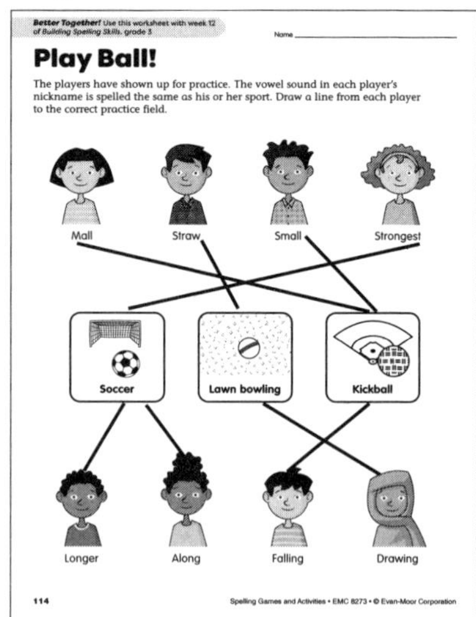

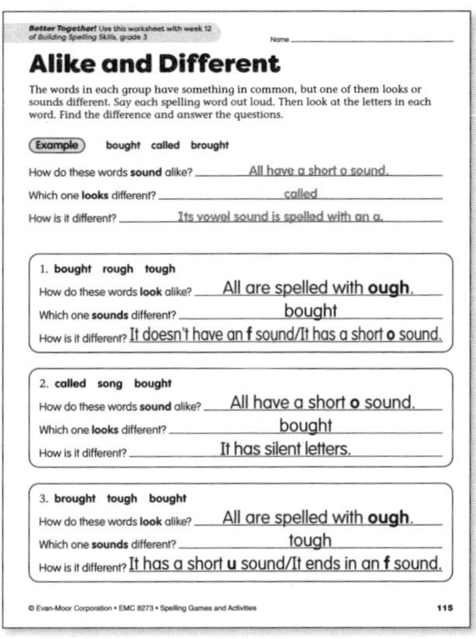

Page 115

Alike and Different

The words in each group have something in common, but one of them looks or sounds different. Say each spelling word out loud. Then look at the letters in each word. Find the difference and answer the questions.

Example   bought   called   brought

How do these words **sound** alike? _All have a short o sound._

Which one **looks** different? _called_

How is it different? _Its vowel sound is spelled with an a._

1. **bought   rough   tough**
How do these words **look** alike? _All are spelled with **ough**._
Which one **sounds** different? _bought_
How is it different? _It doesn't have an **f** sound/It has a short **o** sound._

2. **called   song   bought**
How do these words **sound** alike? _All have a short **o** sound._
Which one **looks** different? _bought_
How is it different? _It has silent letters._

3. **brought   tough   bought**
How do these words **look** alike? _All are spelled with **ough**._
Which one **sounds** different? _tough_
How is it different? _It has a short **u** sound/It ends in an **f** sound._

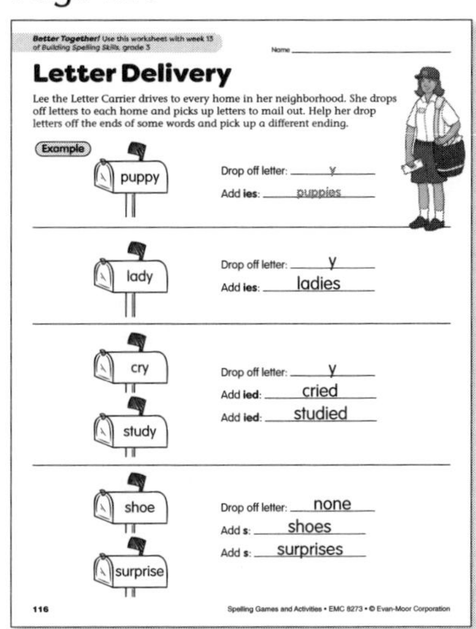

Page 116

Letter Delivery

Lee the Letter Carrier drives to every home in her neighborhood. She drops off letters to each home and picks up letters to mail out. Help her drop letters off the ends of some words and pick up a different ending.

Example   puppy — Drop off letter: _y_   Add **ies**: _puppies_

lady — Drop off letter: _y_   Add **ies**: _ladies_

cry — Drop off letter: _y_   Add **ied**: _cried_
study — Add **ied**: _studied_

shoe — Drop off letter: _none_   Add **s**: _shoes_
surprise — Add **s**: _surprises_

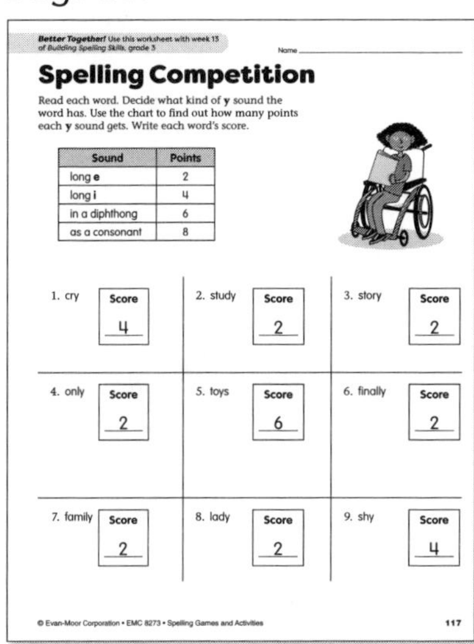

Page 117

Spelling Competition

Read each word. Decide what kind of **y** sound the word has. Use the chart to find out how many points each **y** sound gets. Write each word's score.

Sound	Points
long **e**	2
long **i**	4
in a diphthong	6
as a consonant	8

1. cry — Score: 4
2. study — Score: 2
3. story — Score: 2
4. only — Score: 2
5. toys — Score: 6
6. finally — Score: 2
7. family — Score: 2
8. lady — Score: 2
9. shy — Score: 4

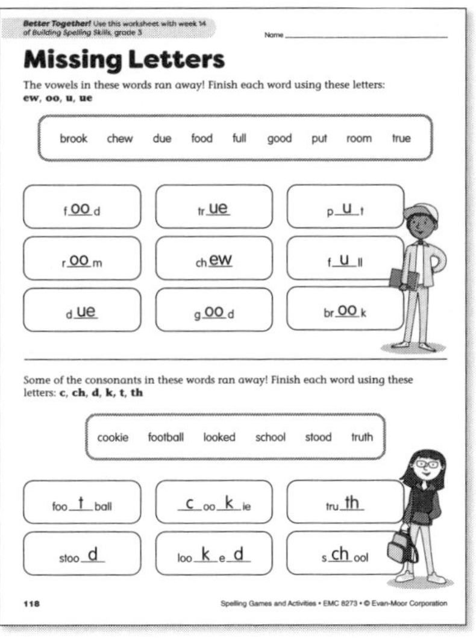

Page 118

Missing Letters

The vowels in these words ran away! Finish each word using these letters: **ew, oo, u, ue**

brook   chew   due   food   full   good   put   room   true

f**oo**d   tr**ue**   p**u**t

r**oo**m   ch**ew**   f**u**ll

d**ue**   g**oo**d   br**oo**k

Some of the consonants in these words ran away! Finish each word using these letters: **c, ch, d, k, t, th**

cookie   football   looked   school   stood   truth

foo**t**ball   **c**oo**k**ie   tru**th**

stoo**d**   loo**k**ed   s**ch**ool

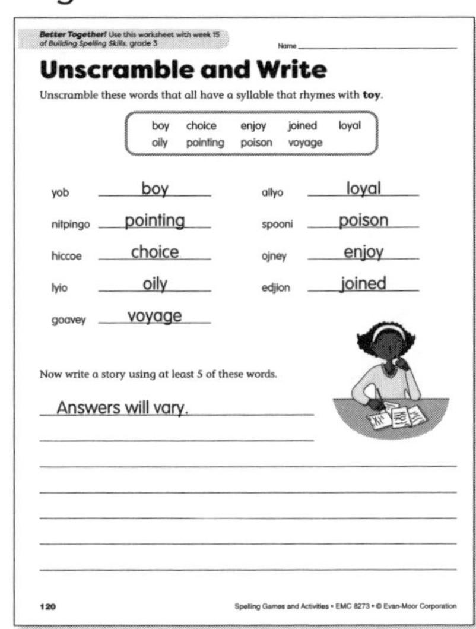

Page 120

Unscramble and Write

Unscramble these words that all have a syllable that rhymes with **toy**.

boy   choice   enjoy   joined   loyal
oily   pointing   poison   voyage

yob — _boy_   allyo — _loyal_
nitpingo — _pointing_   spooni — _poison_
hiccoe — _choice_   ojney — _enjoy_
lyio — _oily_   edjion — _joined_
goavey — _voyage_

Now write a story using at least 5 of these words.

Answers will vary.

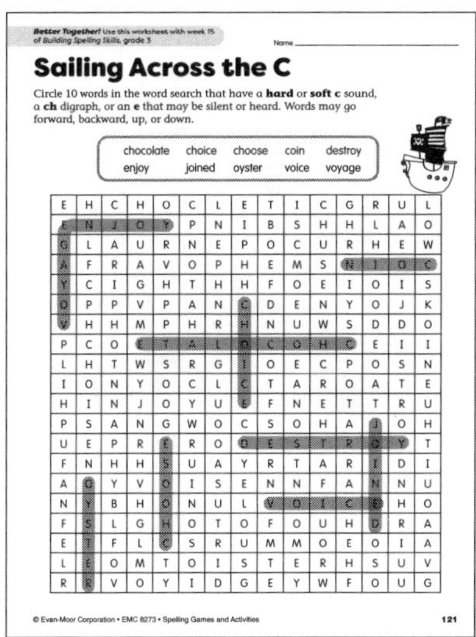

Page 121

Sailing Across the C

Circle 10 words in the word search that have a **hard** or **soft c** sound, a **ch** digraph, or an **e** that may be silent or heard. Words may go forward, backward, up, or down.

chocolate   choice   choose   coin   destroy
enjoy   joined   oyster   voice   voyage

Page 122

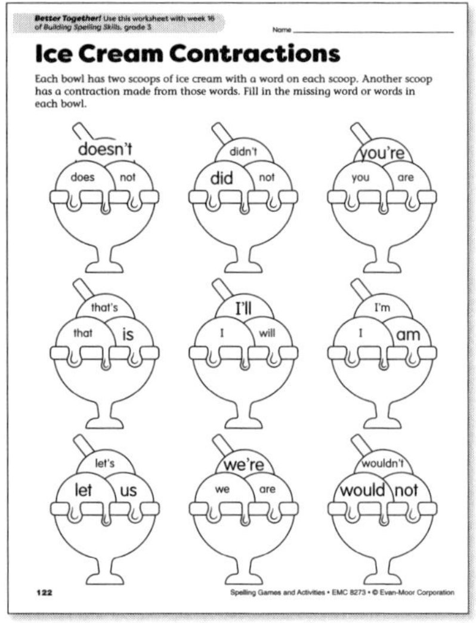

Page 123

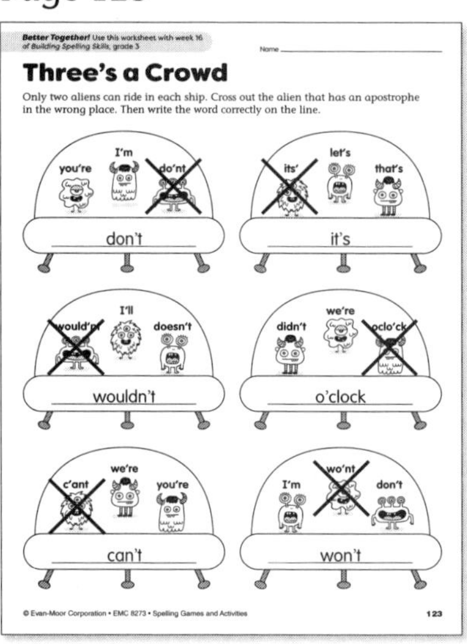

Page 124

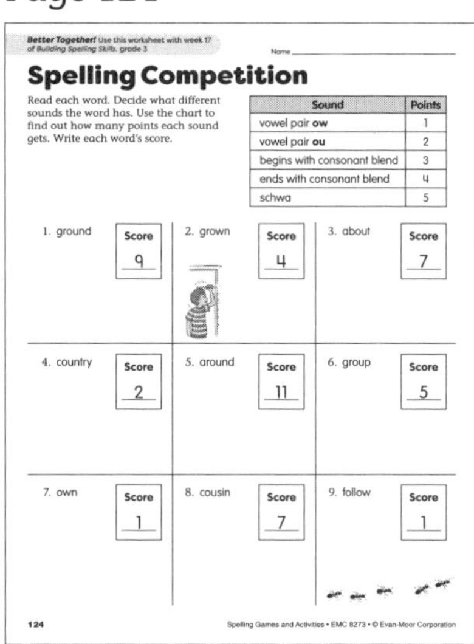

Page 125

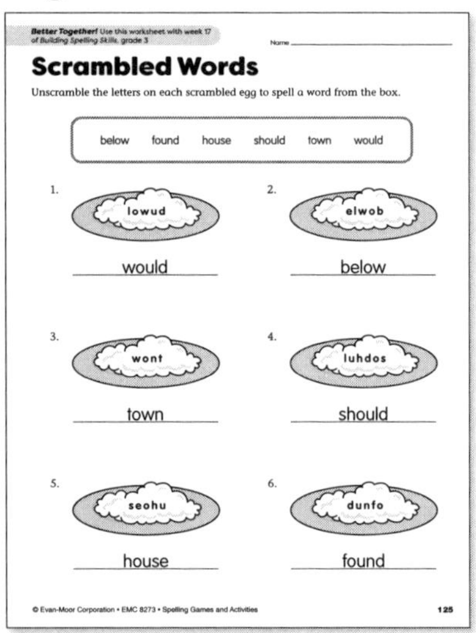

Page 126

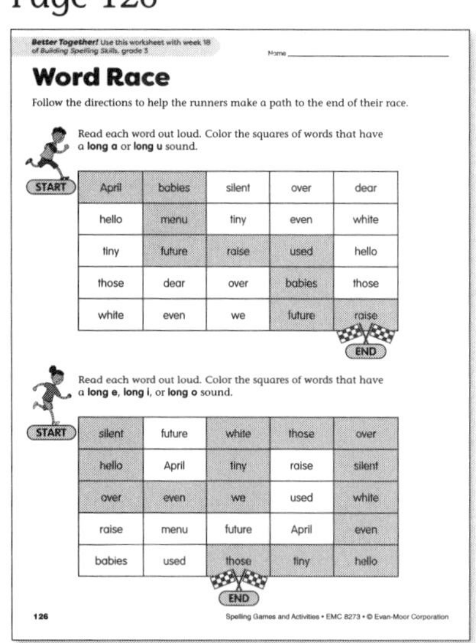

Page 127

Page 128

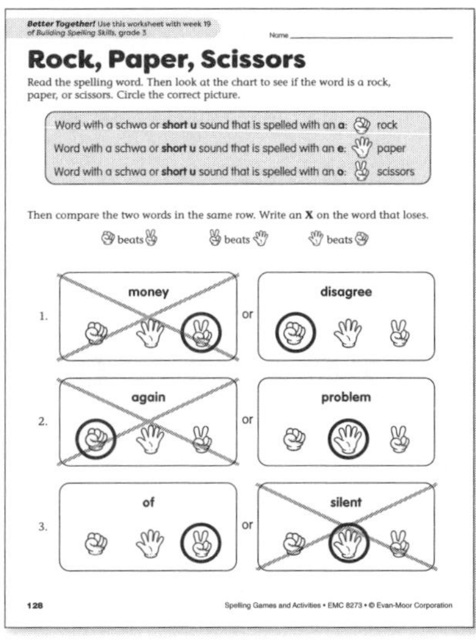

Page 130

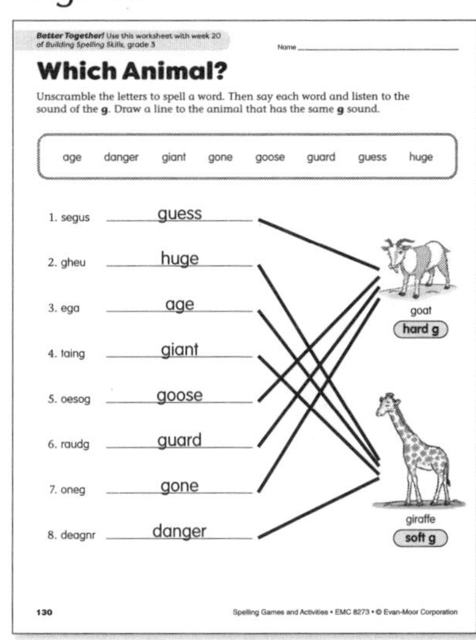

Page 131

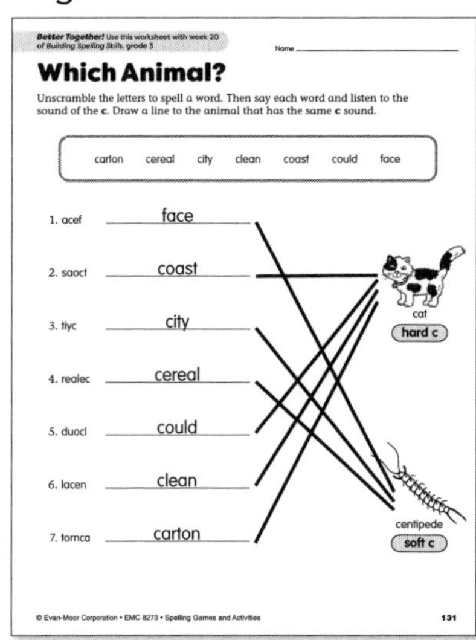

Page 132

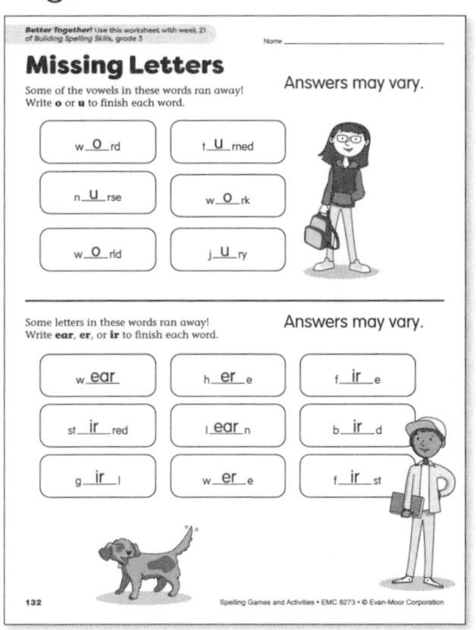

Page 133

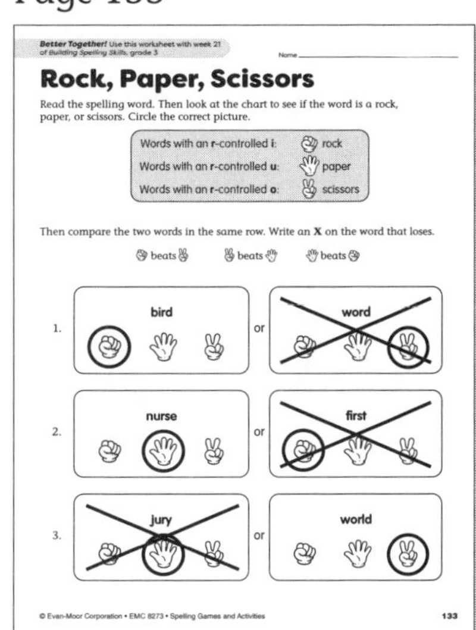

Page 134

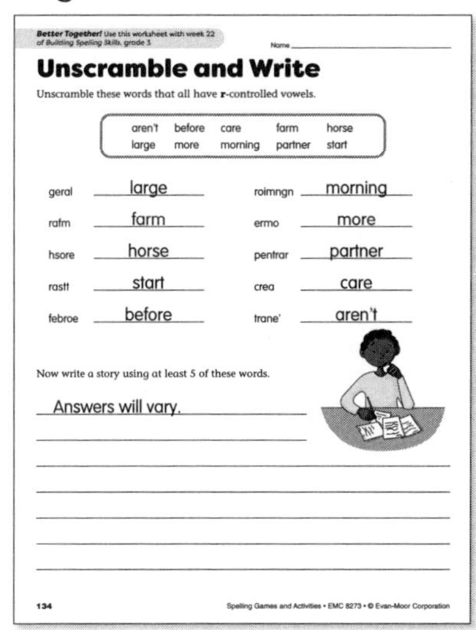

Page 135

Page 136

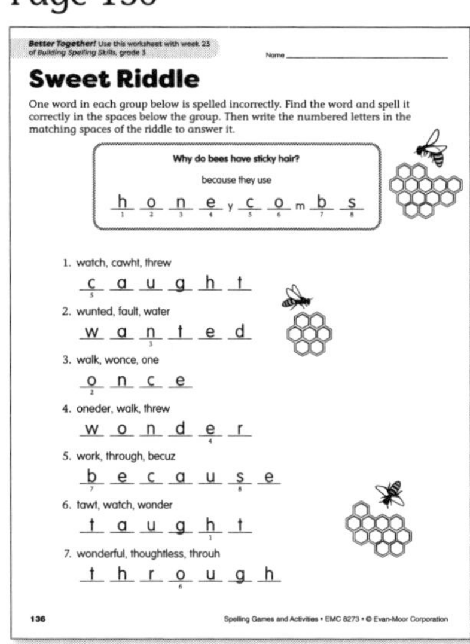

Page 137

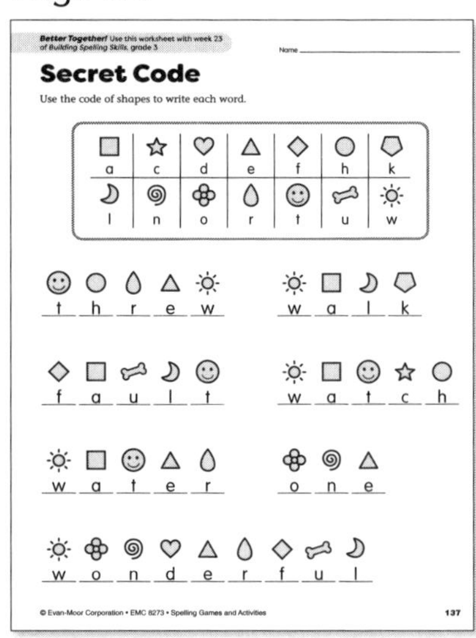

Page 138

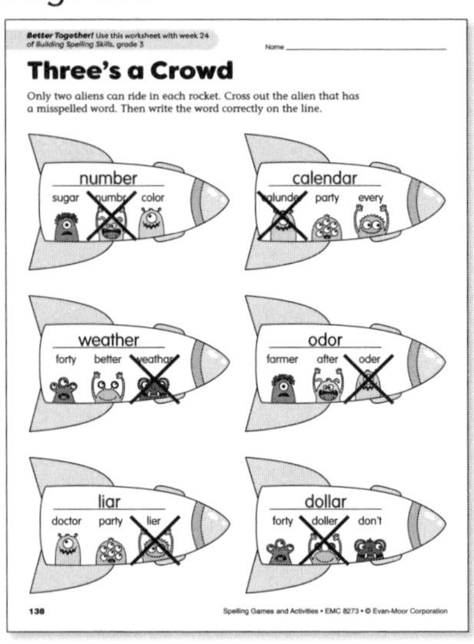

Page 139

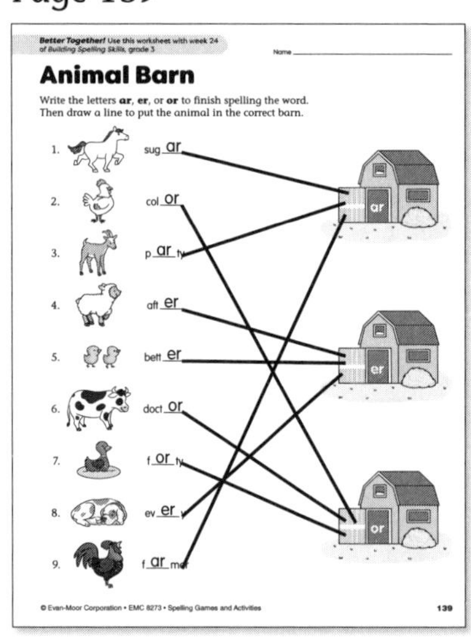

Page 140

Page 141

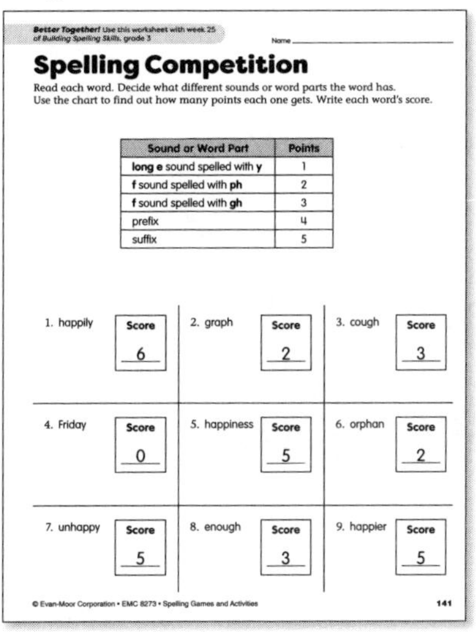

Page 142

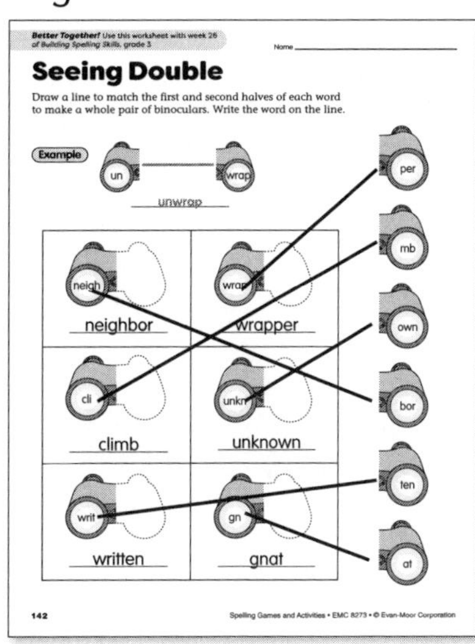

Page 144

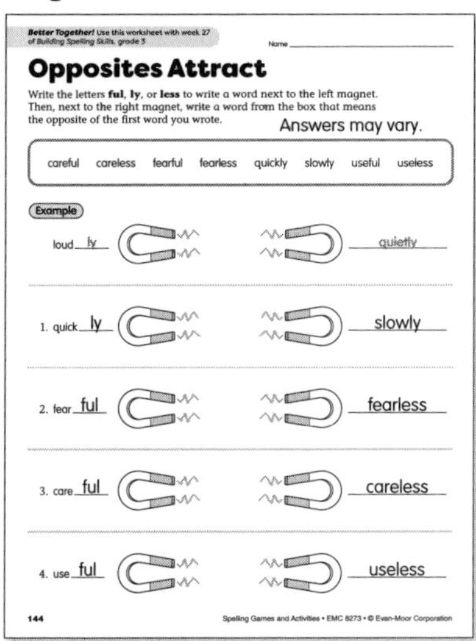

Page 145

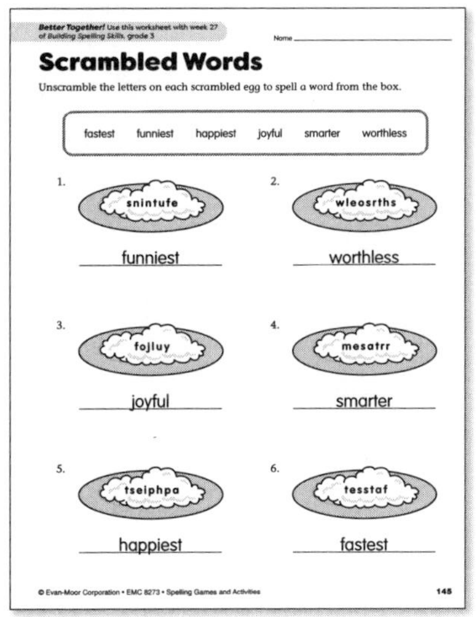

Page 146

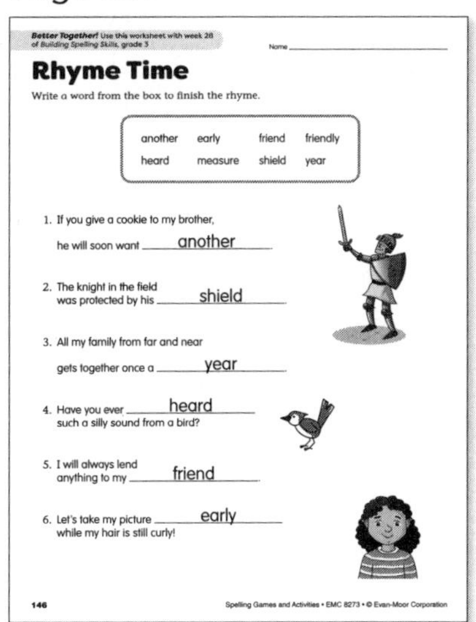

Page 147

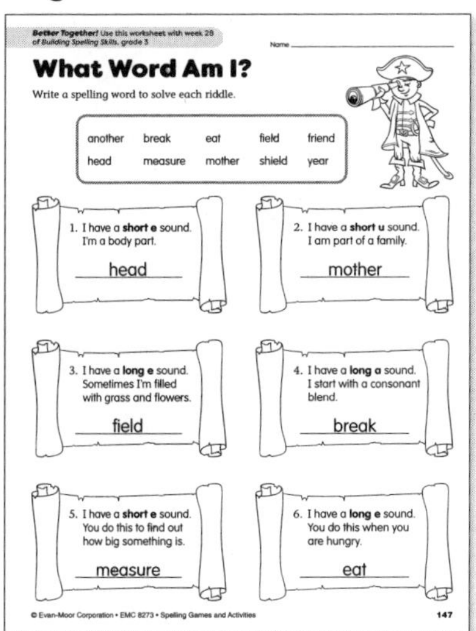

Page 148

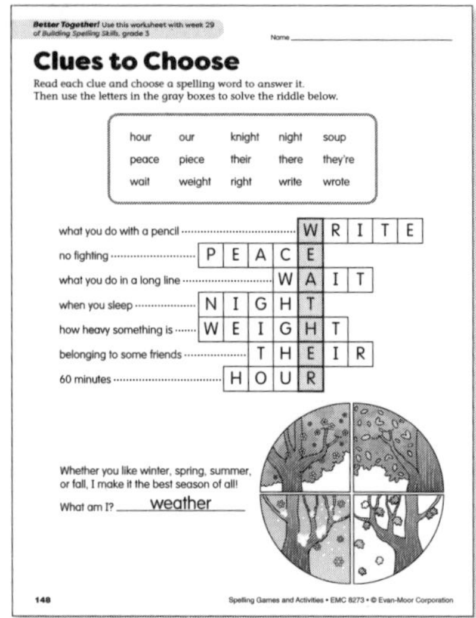

Page 149

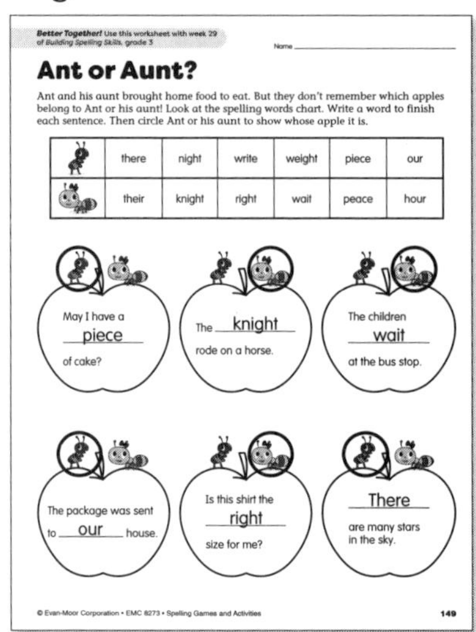

Page 151

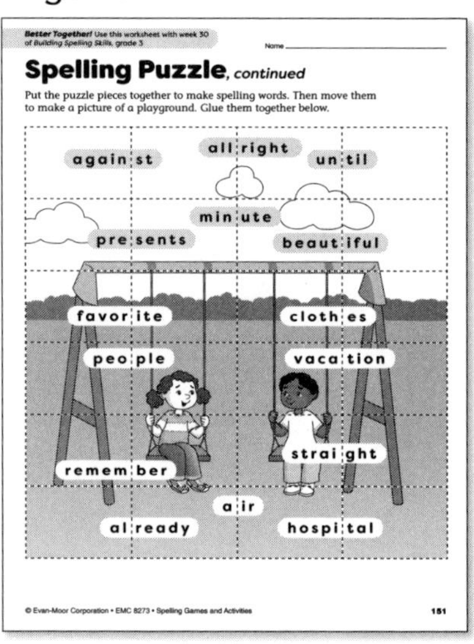